A Guide to Customary Marriage

Among the Jorquelleh Kpelle People

A Guide to Customary Marriage

Among the Jorquelleh Kpelle People

Davidson Sumo

Village Tales Publishing

MINNEAPOLIS, MN

A catalog record for this book is available from the Library of Congress:
Library of Congress Control Number: 2021914520
ISBN: 9781945408755
eISBN: 9781945408748

Published By:
Village Tales Publishing
Minneapolis, MN 55429

Layout and Cover Design by: OASS
www.villagetales.com
www.villagetalespublishing.com

Printed in the United States of America

Dedication

Let me take this time to dedicate my work to my late mother, Ma Gorpu Sumo, who departed this world three years ago due to a prolonged illness. As a child, you nourished me very well and took good care of me. You saved my life on many occasions when I was on my way to face danger as an innocent child.

You were always caring for your children; this is why you never left us behind one day to go ahead on the farm or in the town. I remembered you carrying one of us on your back with the heavy load on your head. Every time, both during the morning and evening hours, to and from the farm, while the rest of us walked in front of you, you watched over us like a mother eagle caring for her eaglets. You used bamboo torchlight to bring us home from the farm when other community dwellers made mockery that you were the only woman that reproduces every year. You sacrificed your life for us when ritualistic killing was rampant in our community during those years of our upbringing.

When my love for you began to grow stronger and deeper, you left us very early in the hands of no other mother like you. When it was time for you to get some return benefits from your children, the cold hand of death struck you down in a foreign land, the most regrettable and unforgettable memory of your demise. I am going to LAC, Grand Bassa County, to visit your siblings was your last conversation with me.

We are who we are today because of you, Mother. My heart pains because of your death. I remembered you and missed you a whole lot during my wedding day when I looked all around and could not see you anywhere by my side.

Thank you, Mother, for our upbringing; may God bless your soul and your children whom you left behind. May your soul rest in perfect peace, Mummy, and keep dreaming of your children. Your memory will live on with us forever and ever. Please send me your pillow that you sleep on so that I can dream of you.

Contents

Acknowledgement

I am very gratified to extend my sincere thanks and appreciations to the following personalities and institutions for their enormous contributions, advice, and supports to our success in this literary work; they include and not limited to my wife and friends for their moral supports, all editors and consultants (Hon. Franklin O. Siakor, Mr. & John Y. Gormuyor) for their pieces of advice and tireless consultancy and editorial works to this endeavor, the Liberian Red Cross, DEN-L and few other organizations for the knowledge and skills acquired and, the employment opportunity afforded us to work and earn income some of which have been directed into this venture to attain success.

My greatest thanks and appreciations go to Jerry Jenkins and Justin Champion (bestselling writers) for their tireless online teaching and mentoring support to me from start to finish. Our success came through their mentorships that will never be forgotten for ages to come.

We are also grateful to Mr. Mulbah T. Jacob, Kerkulah Nuatomue, Ma Nyamah Nanhnon, Mulbah Sulonteh, Ma Korto, Ma Gorlikawuan, Kwelleegbo Kapu, Timothy K. Morris, Sunday T. Mulbah, John F. Locula, Sekou Sirleaf, Paul K. Ricks, and Earnest Siakor, for their brilliant knowledge and vast worth of experiences provided on the prescribed steps and procedures for customary marriage among the Jorquelleh Kpelle people. We've reached the mountain top because of you, so we are very proud of you all.

Thank you.

Preface

Biblically, marriage is a special and unique ceremony that brings together two persons of the opposite sex as husband and wife. This happens all around the world, including Liberia and in Bong County at large. The concept of marriage began in the Garden of Eden with God himself as the master of the ceremony for the union between Adam and Eve. Adam and his wife copied some significant steps and procedures from God and passed them on to their children, Cain, Abel, and Seth. The generations of Abraham, Moses, Isaac, Noah, Ismael, Cain, Enoch, Jacob, Joseph, etc., also experienced their form of marriage. Their generations and many others used these procedures before reaching us. Marriage was not designed between a man and another man, nor a woman and another woman, but created between a man and woman. This is evident by the creation of the woman out of the rib of the man called Adam, contrary to what happened in the days of Sodom and Gomorrah. Genesis 4:17 alludes to the marriage between a man and a woman when Cain loved his wife Awan or Avan and begat Enoch. They were charged with the responsibilities to love, care, respect, and support each other till death do them part. God's intent for marriage was not to be like the case of Sodom and Gomorrah in biblical times. This is one of the many unholy reasons why God destroyed Gomorrah.

Gradually, these early procedures or steps have been duplicated or modified from one generation to another because the culture is not static. We have noticed that we modern men and women of the progressive generation have been adding (mixing up) more values and flavors to our customary marriages (CMs) to suit our needs and current reality.

On the other hand, it is also observed that we modern people are seriously leaving out (subtracting) some essential values and features that have been practiced and kept by our forefathers who lived before us. These values and characteristics have kept our traditions so special and unique even up to the present day. Based on the "add and subtract" factors mentioned above, our original traditional practices related to customary marriages gradually lose their fundamental values and respect as part of the emerging consequences and undermine our initial chronological steps and procedures. Though the steps vary from one tradition to another, every custom has a fixed format for customary marriage ceremonies in terms of practices across the globe.

A second primary reason for the decline in the tradition's practices, including customary marriage procedures, is the oral nature of the heritage. Since customary marriage practices are not written, the tendency of fading out or wearing away is practically imminent. Historians believed that written accounts are better than oral because the contents are usually being added or subtracted as time goes by in the former.

Chronology of the steps involved with customary marriage is gradually wearing away from the ceremonial processes among the Kpelle ethnic group as observed over the years because they are not written.

A third negative effect on customary marriage is the lack of or limited knowledge among the younger and older people on the different and necessary steps that are prescribed and required of the tradition to have a complete ceremony through which a groom can take his bride's hand as his wife. The Bible says, "Where there is no vision, the people perish." This part of our traditional practices may perish if we don't do the needful action to save the culture.

According to our research findings, which have influenced us to write what we have, the fourth major cause that influenced our writing is that the elderly or the older people are not teaching the younger ones who should be taking over from them when they can no longer perform the task due to old age. On the other hand, the young people are very reluctant to ask for or inquire useful information from their parents. As such, the original format or protocol for customary or traditional marriage (TM) is gradually disappearing, and the consequences thereof may cause us to lose our tradition that might be overtaken by western ideology, probably before or at the end of this century.

A fifth major cause for the missteps in the processes leading to customary marriage is the introduction and utilization of the procedures and practices of western marriage into customary marriage. This is done to make a big-big show, gain prestige, and prove how potential a person or a couple is. It is realized that we have given more consideration to the procedures and ingredients of western marriage ideology than ours whenever we are performing customary marriage in our setting in general in Liberia. The Kpelle tribe is no exception. From my analytical point of view, we provide 60% space for the use of the procedures and protocol of western marriage ideology while the remaining 40% is given to our customary marriage procedures into our customary marriages. In other words, we are paying more attention to our negligence and Western ideology whenever we are performing customary marriages. The question is, why should we neglect our own way of life? Western education and western Christianity teach us that our culture is uncivilized, heathen, and barbaric. But is this the reality? Some people may answer yes because of our attitudes. But our culture is neither barbaric nor uncivilized because I hold the view that civilization began in Africa.

The problem is that our attitudes are entirely confirmative with what Chinua Achebe said. Achebe wrote a book and captioned it as "Things Fall Apart-The Center Cannot Hold." Indeed, this is very true that things have fallen apart and that the center can no longer hold. Quite frankly, things have fallen apart in all aspects of our African societies and even within our traditions and our customary marriages. The center can no longer hold. This is why we have lost most of the customary marriage ingredients that are considered approved or required steps to have a complete traditional marriage. Today, most of us cannot independently handle and complete a traditional marriage without being stranded in the process because of our limitations concerning the lack of knowledge about the procedures.

If we want to make a comeback, we need to find out for ourselves in many ways, including maintaining what our custom has provided for our customary use. This sequential gap of customary marriage procedures is being created within our tradition since the introduction of western ideas. We hope to fill this gap and to put ourselves back on track.

As the Kpelle ethnic group is the largest tribe in Liberia, it is very glaring that we are gradually losing grip on the original steps and procedures initially designed and required to perform a complete customary marriage in the Kpelle fashion and elsewhere. This is evident because the many customary marriages conducted in our presence at different time intervals, different venues, and locations in Bong County were somehow handled without uniformity, according to our observation.

This book is primarily written to dig up hidden causes of the wrong applications of our tradition, relative to customary marriage procedures, with the anticipation to help us make a vigorous comeback and remain on track of our traditional marriage procedures and teach future generations to maintain the tradition. There is no one without origin, and so we, the Kpelle ethnic group, have to go back to our roots/routes though the tradition is not static.

One important thing that has been encouraged among us is intermarriage. This has gone a long way in the improvement of the culture for a better future. As we promote intermarriage, the custom of the female counterparts must be highly respected and used in all of our customary wedding ceremonies, which will help in rebuilding these missing links that are crippling the original customary marriage procedures. What is damaging or destroying the fabrics of our traditional marriages is the misapplication of the practice and procedures. This is because either one or both members of the couple coming together hails from different ethnic groups or families and backgrounds that are almost incompatible.

Instead of using the custom of the bride who is being married, the groom's family will try to impose their will on the ceremony being conducted or blend them both. For instance, some families will insist that the groom's family hosts the marital ceremony instead of the bride's family, while others will compel the groom's family to buy the child/children between them that were born out of wedlock before the dowry payment. In some cases, others will insist that the amount of $10.00USD be paid to the bride's family for damage done to the home (sex before dowry payment). Since the two or more practices do not agree with other customary marriages in other traditions, conflict is inevitable because we are not culturally tolerant. Borrow, add and subtract ideologies have become the order of our traditional marriage for this and past generations. These and many other reasons mentioned above have provoked us to propound just what we are reading today.

There are three main seeds of germination used as a catalyst in the successful development of this full-grown manuscript. In other words, the methodologies used to gather and grow useful data and materials for the compilation of this book include direct observations, interviews with key informants (KIs), and direct participation of the writer into several customary marriages as a way of practicing and understanding how to conduct traditional marriage ceremonies across Bong County.

In a nutshell, there is no homogeneity or consistency in the current practical use of our customary procedures for marriage. Should this continue? The big answer is, no and so let's read and see.

Introduction

A Guide to Customary Marriage takes its title and theme from the current status quo of our customary marriage ceremony handlings across Liberia. The present ritual related to the practices of the steps and procedures of our traditional ceremonies seems to go contrary to what our forefathers established and practiced many generations before us. The manipulation or crafting of the book's title comes from how our culture, especially the customary marriage procedure, is being wrongly handled or practiced by us. The procedures are now misguided, misapplied, and misused; our generation is seriously forgetting, ignoring, and incorrectly applying traditional marriage techniques in Liberia, especially in Bong County among the Jorquelleh Kpelle tribe. When these misguided practices of our traditional marriage continue, our marriage procedures will eventually wipe out as it is already under threat to phase out. A Guide to Customary Marriage is written to erect the checkpoint and remind us that a significant component of the tradition is on the verge of collapse. We must act immediately to reawaken it right now. Amalgamating our efforts and resources into gathering facts on the prescribed procedures and arranging them into chronological order for our use and the use of future generations is our primary focus.

As we practice customary marriage in Liberia, especially among the Kpelle ethnic group, it is essential to know the various necessary steps and procedures that are prescribed and required to obtain a bride through our tradition. Furthermore, these procedures must be practiced with consistency to maintain uniformity among the people of the Kpelle tribe.

This book is mended to help us restore our already dying culture, which will help us understand how our people lived and married in time. Modern people can learn and uphold our standard and original traditional marriage procedures from one generation to another. We must establish or differentiate traditional marriage procedures from western or statutory marriage. This will always keep us on track to avoid deviation that may eventually trigger the wearing away and eliminate the tradition and practices that seem very dear to the Kpelle tradition.

This book (Guide to Customary Marriage) is written solely about how the Kpelle people—the Jorquelleh Kpelle tribe—can conduct their customary marriage, bringing together a man and a woman as husband and wife. The book's focus is placed on the steps and procedures prescribed and required for a groom to marry his bride in line with our tradition. From our investigation, it is established that the custom of the bride has always been used during customary marriages instead of the groom's tradition. The groom is going away to the woman's home and her parents to look for what he did not lose. In this case, we do not expect the groom's custom to prevail over or overshadow the entire ceremony as he struggles as a stranger in this place to find his lifetime partner. But this is not the case in our current marriages due to our ignorance, selfishness, power, greed, biggity, and modification methods as civilized people as we call ourselves. The problem here is that we have acculturated and taught the practices of foreign ideologies and procedures into our customary marriages, a situation that has brought us thus far.

The Jorquelleh Kpelle tribe is singled out in this book because the Kpelle language under discussion has several versions, including the Jorquelleh Kpelle, Salala/Gibi Kpelle,

Sanoyea Kpelle, Zota/Jota Kpelle, Kokoyah Kpelle, Bopolu Kpelle, and the Guinea Kpelle, amongst others. Since there are several strata of the Kpelle language in Liberia, Bong County, Guinea, and elsewhere, the steps, procedures, or protocols discussed herein are concentrated on the custom and tradition of the Jorquelleh Kpelle ethnic group, which has many things in common with the other versions except the variation in pronunciations, accent and attitudes of the people at times.

The book places more emphasis on the step-by-step procedures during the customary wedding. It teaches us which activity comes first, second, third, and so on until the last activity before and after taking the bride's hand. Within the sustainability chapter, you will learn how to practice and maintain our customary marriage procedures in an orderly manner.

The book incorporates seven chapters in all. Chapters one and two focus on the definition, legality, and the general overview of customary and statutory marriages. Western marriage's influence and consequences on customary marriage are detailed in the third chapter, while the prescribed basic steps and procedures are outlined in the fourth chapter. Chapter five deals with the entire dowry payment, and chapter six teaches us about the sustainability of our tradition, emphasizing the procedures of our customary marriage. Within the sustainability chapter, you will learn how to practice and maintain our customary marriage procedures in an orderly manner to serve as a heritage for us.

And finally, in the last chapter (ch.7), the book will help you clearly understand how to conduct customary marriage through a practical step-by-step model or illustration concerning a bride and her groom, beginning with step one (the engagement) to step two, the dowry payment and down to the last step (the farewell package presentation). Thus, chapter seven is the final chapter designed to translate or transform chapter four from theory to practice. In other words, the prescribed basic steps and procedures narrated in chapter four have been transformed from theory to action through a practical model borrowed from a real-life traditional marriage ceremony between a bride and her groom.

Please take your time to read carefully and attentively to enjoy the book. It is very educative, informative, entertaining, inspiring, and attractive.

A young married couple.

Chapter One

The Definitions & Legality of Statutory Marriage versus Customary Marriage

In Biblical terms, marriage is defined as a process through which a man shall leave his father and mother and cleave unto his wife, and they shall become one flesh according to Scriptures (Genesis 2:24). In this case, the partners involved are covenanting their life together in sickness and health, for better, for worse until death parts them. Marriage is matrimony designed by God to bring together a male and female into one union as husband and wife. The primary intent of the union is to reproduce after their kind, for sexual pleasure, for happiness, and worship or service to God (biblical interpretation).

Sociologists define marriage as a socially supported union involving two or more individuals in what is regarded as a stable, enduring arrangement typically based at least in part on a sexual bond of some kind. It is also a social contract between a man and a woman that blends their lives in one union.

Contrary to the above concepts, practices, and protocols, the parents of the groom among the Kpelle tribe have the responsibility to leave and search for a bride for their son; and then unite them into one union as husband and wife at the age of maturity, which is typically determined by them (the parents).

Tradition is defined as the transmission of customs or beliefs from one generation to another generation or the fact of being passed on in this way. Custom is a traditional and widely accepted form of behaving or doing something specific to a particular society, place, or time.

In the old days, the parents were responsible for seeking and choosing their daughter's husband for marriage. Parents were also obligated to find and choose their son's wife for life, as earlier stated. This is why when a man or boy, for marriage, approached a girl child, she never agrees immediately. Instead, she consults the mother, and the mother will also reach out to the girl's father. These parents will decide to accept or reject the proposal because they knew precisely the background of the family who wants to marry their daughter.

But as civilization improves, laws were made and enforced to protect the rights of everyone. One of such laws is the "Equal Rights of the Customary Marriage Law of 1998 and 2003. Chapter 2, section 2.1 accords equal rights to customary wives like in a statutory wife case. This means that both kinds of marriages have equal values and rights. However, in the same chapter, section 2.10, it is unlawful for parents to choose their daughter's husband. This law prohibits parents from making the marital decision for their child/children. The law says that this is a first-degree felony accompanied by a particular fine. Additionally, section 2.4 prohibits compulsory wife labor, while section 2.8 forbids unlawful confession of the name of suspected boyfriend by a customary wife instead of ancient days customary practices.

The concept and interpretation among the traditional people probably for choosing a wife for their son might have been copied from the days of creation when God Himself made a woman (wife) for Adam out of his rib bone. In this case, it was not Adam who chose for himself a wife but rather God his father. The Bible says, *"And so the Lord God caused the man to fall into sleep; and while he (Adam) was sleeping, He took one of the man's ribs and then closed up the place with flesh. Then the Lord made a woman from the rib He had taken out of the man, and He brought her to the man."* (Genesis 2:21-22 NIV) When Adam awoke, God said unto him, *"And this is your wife (helpmate), she is now the bone of your bones and flesh of your flesh; she shall be called woman."* In this case, it was not Adam who searched for his wife but rather God, his father. And so, in a nutshell, it was God the father who searched, and Adam received. This might have been the tradition still rolling on to the present but is now on the verge of collapse among the Kpelle tribe based on the "add and subtract factors" that I have observed and mentioned earlier in the introduction.

The Constitution of Liberia gives equal rights to all citizens of Liberia, including the right to marry at the age of 18 years and above. According to the Act on Equal Rights of the Customary Marriage Law of 1998, customary marriages and statutory marriages are both equal before and under the Liberian law (see chapter 2, Section 2.1 of the Equal Rights of Customary Marriage Law of 1998), which accords equal rights to both statutory and customary wives. The law clarifies that one statute cannot override another statute; only the constitution can render a statute void. "All customary marriage shall be legal within this Republic." According to the Equal Rights Marriage Law, both husband and wife are entitled to each other's property at death. But the Equal Rights of Customary Marriage Law does not have specifications for divorce, although it posits the equalization of both marriages. The absence of a legal remedy or means for customary wives or any parties to a divorce is a significant omission in the law.

Notwithstanding this flaw, in actual practice, suggests that a man can return a woman to her family, and this will serve as an official divorce in line with the tradition. In the past, a man could recover dowry paid from his bride's family if he wanted to terminate the relationship or return the woman to the family, which would be the end of the relationship. But currently, the customary marriage law prohibits the recovery of dowry. It states that *"if a husband demands recovery of dowry, it is a first-degree felony and that is indictable or punishable by law."*

Marriage by Presumption:

The marriage presumption doctrine is a common-law marriage; it is a form of marriage conferred on couples based on their conduct. This form of marriage gets its credibility from the endorsement of family, friends, and the community. The validity of marriage presumption is decided through judicial decisions. Marriage presumption grants legal marital status to cohabitants who uphold themselves as husband and wife. These cohabitants assume marital status upon themselves even though their union was not formally solemnized or licensed. Typical factors that motivate couples to see themselves as a married couple are procreation and raising children, sharing/bearing last name, common investment, listing each other as the beneficiary on insurance, employment, real property, and other crucial or essential documents, like the management of finances. In the absence of a dispute, the legality of the relationship is not an issue.

Any husband who collects or attempts to collect dowry from his wife or her parents using force, directly or indirectly, has committed a felony of the first degree. Upon conviction in a court of competent jurisdiction, shall be fined the amount of not less than LD500.00 and not more than LD1,000.00, including restitution, if any dowry was refunded according to the same Act under discussion.

Marriage by presumption is the third category of marriage recognized under Liberian Law. Therefore, beware of such marriage and try hard to put things right, either traditionally, legally, or religiously. In my analysis of this third category of marriage, I placed the chances of any of the partners losing or gaining proceeds from such partnership when conflict arises or when death occurs at a ratio of 50:50 win-win or win-lose ratio because the whole world is more legal than ever.

Interestingly, it is very glaring to note that Liberians, and the rest of the world, have divided marriage into two conventionally accepted categories and termed them customary marriage and western or statutory marriage.

Customary marriage, also known as traditional marriage, is when a male and a female come together as husband and wife through a special traditional ceremony performed locally among certain groups of people, tribes, nations, and regions. This process is a common practice handed down from one generation to another. Usually, this is performed by family heads, elders, and other high-profile family members or dignitaries in a given society like the Kpelle tribe in Bong County. During such a ceremony, culture plays a significant role in the entire process.

Western marriage is the modern form of matrimony instituted by God himself to bring together a groom and the bride (Adam-the male & Eve-the female) in the garden, the church, or religious terrain. But humankind uses the court, hall, beach, or other non-religious open landscapes where the couple exchanges vow and rings. This kind of wedding is derived from the western world like America, Great Britain, France, Germany, Italy, etc.

Another name for western marriage is statutory or civil marriage. The main focus of Western Marriage is placed on the legal and spiritual or religious bases as the fulcrum. During this type of marriage, documents like licenses & certificates are signed and attested to validate the legality of the union. In biblical or spiritual fulfillment of such union, the wedding is usually done at the church and spearheaded by a clergyman on religious ground. They play the lead role in exchanging vows and rings as an endorsement or confirmation. In fulfillment of the legal aspect of such marriage, the court is most often used to conduct the wedding, followed by the signing of certificates and licenses by all the major stakeholders involved. This aspect, too, is usually handled by a legal practitioner on legal grounds.

Other forms and practices of modern marriage include Homosexualism, lesbianism, and transgender systems of marriage, which are not the focus of this book. Nevertheless, these relationships are highlighted to authenticate the argument further that we are adding to and subtracting some values to and from the prescribed procedures of our customary marriage. These are mentioned because they are believed to be some of the major factors responsible for the breaks and changes within the practices of our traditional marriages.

A homosexual is a person who is sexually attracted to people of their own sex. Homo is a prefix that means one or same. It also refers to modern man (Homo sapiens). It is a Latin word that means man (www.vocabulary.com). Homosexuality is common among men. In this case, one of the two men will choose to submit sexually and in everything as the woman or wife while the other will serve or play the man's role or the husband in the relationship.

Lesbians are two females agreeing to intermarry to understand that one member is the man and the other is the woman.

Transgender is a system of informed consent wherein a person agrees to change their original genital organ with an opposite one through surgical means. For instance, a man willingly consented to extract his penis and replaced it with a vagina or female sexual organ. Likewise, a female replaced her vagina with a penis by surgical means. However, we must admit that these practices are detrimental and foreign to the practice and sustainability of our dear custom among the Kpelle people.

Biologically, a female who changed her organ to a male organ might never reproduce because specific organs and hormones are not changed during the surgery. Ovaries in females and testes in the male are central organs for reproduction in human. Can these organs be changed (replaced) a hundred percent during the surgery to promote reproduction in the case of transgender? Let us take a look at some of the medical facts and implications.

Transgender individuals who undergo gender-affirming medical or surgical therapies are at risk for infertility. Suppression of puberty with gonadotropin-releasing hormone agonist analogs (GnRHa) in the pediatric transgender patient can pause the maturation of sperm cells and thus, affect fertility potential. Testosterone therapy in transgender men can suppress ovulation and alter ovarian histology, while estrogen therapy in transgender women can lead to impaired spermatogenesis and testicular atrophy. The effect of hormone therapy on fertility is potentially reversible, but the extent is unclear. Gender-affirming surgery (GAS) that includes hysterectomy and oophorectomy in transmen or orchiectomy in transwomen results in permanent sterility (barrenness). It is recommended that clinicians counsel transgender patients on fertility preservation (FP) options before initiating gender-affirming therapy. Transmen can choose to undergo. (Trans/Andro/.2019 Jun., Benjamin 1964)

My advice to all would-be candidates for transgender decisions is; don't fool yourself, stop defying nature to your detriment. It is not only the genital organs that make you a man or a woman. Your strength, structure, mentality, ears, fingers & toes, walking, voice, etc., are also essential things and areas that need to be changed to convince the world that you are now a different person in terms of gender. *"It is only the stubborn fly that follows the corpse to the grave."* (Nigerian adage). But you have to remember that this type of fly is always buried along with the carcass. If the level plain field is created for these human interactions among us Kpelle people, there is a high risk of wiping out our marriage system because of its monetary value attached to it. Money can do anything to open any door to achieve a desired goal. Money is one of the factors influencing the misapplication of the processes leading to customary marriage.

Whether the marriage is customary or western, both good sides are legally recognized and accepted by the government of a given country and the church, like in our case in Liberia. Both are equally equal before the law. Conversely, customary or traditional marriage does allow the man to take the hand of another woman, or women, as his wife/wives according to the tradition in Liberia, without interference from the current wife or wives because there is a legal provision as a backup. As opposed to western marriage, the church and the law of Liberia do not allow the man or husband to take a second wife or more unless one of the partners or couple dies or divorces legally. But outside the church and the court, a traditional husband can marry more than one wife according to our custom without legal implications.

As Liberian couples enjoy the beauties of customary and statutory marriages, double marriage has become a common practice among us. In my own words, double-marriage is defined as the combination and the usage of customary and western marriages by a couple one after the other. Such an act, in my prediction, has the propensity to come into conflict with the laws governing the two types of marriages in the future because of its nature of double-marriage when there was no divorce after the first one, which is always the traditional marriage. Therefore, my advice to all incoming couples is that we must be cautious because the interpretation of this is to marry a woman two times. And if you get married twice, beware of the future legal implications when things go wrong. Remember that the Liberian law endorses customary marriage and statutory marriage equally. And so, if you apply both in the case of one woman or a bride, I termed it as a double-marriage (marrying one woman two times).

When the going gets tough, you might be caught up in the web of marital conflict one day. You shall be compelled to undo one of the two marriages that you have already undergone before winning a legal case in your favor in a court of competent jurisdiction. The analysis here is that if a situation may cause you to decide to divorce your partner, which of the two types of marriages will you prefer to divorce when the two are equal? Or will you divorce two times as you did with double-marriage? Will a Liberian court honor a double divorce for you couple? I guess that the answer lies right within our power as we venture into marriage. Double-marriage is increasing because of the changes within the culture compared to the past when traditional marriage was most popular while civil marriage was scanty.

Let us surmise that a married couple gets into a marital conflict; the case is taken to court, and a hearing is conducted with one party being guilty. Probably the western marriage case scenario was used to sue. It is possible that one of the parties involved can lose the first case in court and can bounce back to issue writ against the other party using the traditional category to satisfy their objective. The question is, will the person be wrong to sue again using one of the two categories?

As you contemplate the above question, I want to sensitize you that all is not lost if you have not yet derived at the appropriate answer to this question above.

According to the Liberia Inheritance Law, especially in the case of double-marriage as I termed it, the law prioritizes, honors, or endorses the first marriage that you did as the legal one that can be used as a trump card for adjudication. This means that if you married the woman traditionally for the first time before marrying her statutorily, the law recognizes the traditional marriage over the western or statutory marriage, provided you did sign a certificate during that marriage. But, on the other hand, suppose you married your wife by statutory means before performing the traditional marriage. In that case, the statutory marriage takes preeminence over the customary type in a court of competent jurisdiction, especially when you allow yourself to sign marriage-related documents according to the Liberia Inheritance Law (input from Mrs. Dorothy K. Toomaan, Gender Expert/DEN-L).

My dear readers, let me acquaint you with some information; there is a secret behind this if you want to find an escape route to this rock and roll drama if you do not want to be caught in the legal web of double-marriage. From my observation of the two types of marriages in Liberia, customary or traditional marriage in recent times has always been the first ceremony conducted among the Kpelle tribe in Liberia. This is always followed by statutory marriage because modern man tries to legalize everything in this dispensation. Therefore, signing marriage certificates, licenses, etc., has become a significant thing for married couples in the modern era. Both partners involved in the marital relationship are well protected and legally saved when they signed these legal documents at the wedding. Since, indeed, this is the case, I strongly advise that you should not sign any matrimonial document when you are conducting your traditional marriage ceremony if you have the plan to do the statutory type. But if you signed, then you have tied yourself legally. Just go ahead and show yourself as husband-to-be though you might fulfill all other formalities required of the tradition during your customary marriage. Since we are modern people as we claim to be, the matrimonial document to sign is the statutory marriage because it is easier and available. But if you like, you can sign the required document (traditional certificate) during your customary marriage ceremony. But remember that if you sign the required documents for statutory marriage during your second wedding (western), the Liberian court will only honor the first wedding certificate you signed and legally accept it as the most authentic relationship (input & advice from Mrs. Tooman).

As we close on this chapter, it is now up to you; to decide which of these two types of marriages you may want to prioritize so that you can take all necessary precautions and then sign all the related documents that will go a long way on your entire legal matrimonial journey that the court can use for adjudication whenever conflict arises in the future.

My valued readers, don't forget to note that conflict with a man (human) is inevitable. According to Dr. Joseph Saye Guannue of the Cuttington University Peace Institute, "*Conflict with man is like the teeth and tongue that live together in the same house (the mouth) but yet clash at times when things go wrong.*" So, as you go about marrying your partner, expect conflict and plan how to manage it. Failure to manage or handle conflict within a matrimonial relationship can eventually lead to legal processes that lead to separation or divorce.

As a peace and development studies student, my advice is to encourage and promote connectors and discourage and reject the dividers. In peace-building, connectors are those things that you can do or say to bring happiness, togetherness, unity, peace, satisfaction, tranquility, etc. Connectors connect or bring partners together and make them more friendly and happy. In addition, these connectors help to build a stronger matrimonial relationship.

Dividers are those things, behaviors, actions, saying, attitudes, vices, etc., that keep partners or people far apart from each other. Dividers are enemies to progress, peace, happiness, satisfaction, and many more vices. Dividers are the best friends to conflict. In summary, dividers do not allow a married couple to have peace of mind and happiness in their matrimonial home.

The lesser the connectors, the greater the dividers, and the lesser the dividers, the greater the connectors in the married home. Once you allow the dividers to overcome your connectors, I'm afraid that legality will take preeminence over the relationship, thus triggering separation or divorce between the husband and the wife. So, beware of the dividers in your married home to avoid legality and promote resolution.

Chapter Two

General Overview of Customary/Traditional Marriage in Liberia

Tradition and custom are most often interchangeably used to understand the way of life and practices of a particular group of people under discussion. The two words are synonymous or interwoven literally. In our deliberations, you might often see the use of the words custom or tradition or the combination of both words expressing one idea.

A marriage may either be endogamous or exogamous. Endogamous marriage requires marriage within the same family, social group, same tribe, same region, etc. An example is a marriage between cousins, nephews, nieces, or extended family members. Exogamous marriage is marriage outside of the same family, social group, same tribe, same region, etc. A marriage between a male and a female of different backgrounds (without family connection) is a vivid example. A marriage between a Liberian and British couple is another good example of exogamous marriage.

In our case, for centuries ago, marriage has been highly endogamous before introducing Western practices into our culture and tradition. But surprisingly for us, exogamous marriage has taken a considerable lead over the other, thus immensely contributing to the missteps and missing links within our customary marriage procedures. For instance, if a Liberian woman is marrying an American man, it is very difficult for the custom and tradition of this woman to be respected because of the mixture of the two foreign cultures into one. In this case, one of the two or a completely new culture will seize the entire sure.

It is believed that the combination of two or more cultures or traditions has the propensity to reproduce something else (another language or culture) because of the different ideas and ways of life. This can be compared to what the painter does to get completely different colors by combining two different colors searching for a neutral color. A typical example is the origin of the Swahili/Kiswahili language in East Africa. The Swahili language is a lingua franca that came into being when Bantu speakers mingled with Arab slavers during the 19th century along the East African Coast (Encyclopedia Britannica). Therefore, once we continue to combine other cultures and traditions with ours, we must expect another or a strange language or culture as a byproduct in the long future.

Whether Customary or Western Marriage, marriage is an institution that took center stage from the days of creation according to scriptures. This has become a common practice everywhere in all parts of the world though in different fashions, forms, and manners. Liberia is no exception, including Bong County, which is the seat of the Kpelle ethnic group under discussion, the largest tribe in the country.

On a general note, there are many different kinds or types of marriages in the world today. These types of marriages depend on the location, region, culture, and society that people find themselves within. The most popular kinds are monogamy, polygamy, polygyny, polyandry, group marriage, etc. Monogamy is the practice of one man marrying one wife. Polygamy is defined as the practice of marrying multiple spouses. Polygyny is a system of marriage in which a male spouse is married to multiple female partners. Polyandry is when a woman is married to more than one husband. Group marriage is also another form of marriage in the world. It is defined as a marriage involving multiple husbands and wives when any man can access any of the wives or vice versa (Wikipedia, www.SociologyGuide.com).

The procedures and steps leading to customary marriage vary from one nation to another, region to region, and from one language or tribe to another tribe.

Among the Kpelle ethnic group, polygamy or bigamy has played a significant role in our traditional marriages even up to the present day. Since our marriage in Liberia is patrimonial (man proposing), polygamous marriage has been deeply rooted in our culture and tradition. In so doing, many men have taken advantage of this opportunity to take on the hands of two, three, or more wives through customary means. It is the western or modern form of marriage that discourages polygamy with monogamy (one man, one woman) as we were told. Monogamy is the most popular form of marriage among the Jorquelleh Kpelle tribe, followed by polygamy. Polyandry is not a common practice among us in Liberia or even in Bong County. Polyandry is a form of marriage in which the female counterpart marries more than one husband.

A man under the traditional laws may contract multiple marriages according to traditions and customs. These marriages are legitimate and solemn under Liberian law (section 2.3 of the equal rights of the customary marriage law). But multiple marriages are forbidden within the church circle and even within the statutory domain despite the tradition. A traditional marriage ceremony includes the engagement of the bride and the payment of dowry to the bride's family. In most Liberian traditional marriages, the dowry consists of the payment of money and the breaking of kola nuts with other valuable items. This has made many traditionalists wrongfully conclude that it is the "price or payment" for the woman, and therefore, consider the woman their property in marriage. This is not true, as speculated. This was the practice of previous generations, which is not compatible with modernity through the laws. At that time, the grooms considered that as the price for buying the woman, and for sure indeed, the bride was sometimes treated like a slave on many occasions. But let me remind you that the bride's price in modern days is the fulfillment of custom and not the buying price for the human being, the bride. There is no price on the scale for selling human beings. In fact, human rights instruments like the Universal Declaration of Human rights (UDHRs) forbids the selling and buying of a human being. Traditional marriages last until death or divorce. The requirement for divorce follows prescribed traditions.

Our nation has two separate but equal value types of marriages called customary or traditional marriage and statutory or civil marriage under Liberian law.

Liberia is comprised of 15 counties or provinces with 16 major tribes or ethnic groups spread across the length and breadth of our beloved country. Each ethnic group has its tradition of customary marriage that is unique to them. Our findings have revealed many similarities, with some tiny differences in how each of these tribes conducts their customary marriage ceremony. For example, the use of kola nuts and the payment of $48.00US are almost practiced by all tribes. According to Alhaji Sekou Sirleaf of Gbarnga, three (3) cows are often used to pay the bride's price within the Mandingo tradition, including kola nuts and money.

Certainly, the groom's family among the Kpelle is charged with a specified amount to buy the child/children between him and the bride before conducting the customary marriage ceremony if they have lived together for some time before marriage. This practice is common among many Liberian tribes. According to traditionalists, this is done to free the children from bondage or slavery to freedom and legal protection according to the modified version of Kpelle tradition. This did not happen among our ancient people because the couple did not know each other sexually or were allowed to reproduce offspring before marriage. An amount of $10.00USD is also paid for a relationship with sexual affairs before marriage. Traditional people called it *fees* for damage done to their daughter against the custom. Customarily, the bride's uncles, commonly known as the muus, usually have complete authority over the money paid for this ultimate affair with their daughter out of wedlock. Other tribes do not practice farewell packages at the close of the customary marriage ceremony like the Kpelle ethnic group. Our 16 Liberian ethnic groups discussed in this chapter include Kpelle, Bassa, Mano, Gio, Krahn, Grebo, Kru, Vai, Gola, Lorma, Kissi/Gissi, Gbandi, Belle, Dei, Mende, and Mandingo.

According to African history, these tribes are grouped into three categories: the Mande, Kwa, and Mel speaking groups. The Mande, sometimes called Mendi, contains the Kpelle, Mende, Gio/Dan, Mano, Vai, Lorma, and Gbandi tribes. These Mande-speaking tribes are primarily found in the northwest and central regions of Liberia. They are also found in Sierra Leone, Mali, Guinea, and Senegal. The Kpelle-speaking tribe is the largest single ethnic group among the Mande-speaking people in Liberia. On the national scene, the Kpelle tribe is also the largest tribe among all the tribes in Liberia, with at least 20.3% of our total population. The Kwa-speaking group is comprised of Bassa, Kru, Grebo, Dei, Belle, and Krahn. The Kwa speakers occupied the southern half of Liberia and were the earliest converts to Christianity. The Mel-speaking people include the Gola and Kissi tribes, respectively. They are found in the north and the coastal region of the northwest. These people are also found in Sierra Leone and are also known to be the oldest inhabitants of Liberia. (Liberia-People/Britannica)

African History tells us that these different ethnic groups might have migrated from western Sudan to find a haven from powerful warriors, warlords, tribal groups, who fought each other for gold, salt, kingdoms, empires, land, slaves for sale, etc. To further authenticate this history of migration, the Kpelle tribe, as a member of the Mende-speaking group, has some things in common with some Liberian tribes. For example, according to my independent investigation, the use and interpretation of the English word "BUT" has similar pronunciation and meaning in some of Liberia's 16 tribes. The Kpelle people called it *"kei/keh,"* which means "but" in conjunctional form. If you do your investigation, you will get to understand that few other Liberian tribes use this *kei/keh* pronunciation in place of the word "but' in their respective tribes, even within the Kwa and Mel speakers. According to

Dolomark Konneh of Bomi County, the Gola ethnic group called it *kei/keh* with the same meaning. The Lorma, Kru, Mano, Bassa, and Mandingo people call it *kei* or *keh*, which means "but" as a conjunction among these tribes according to Johnson Kesselly, J. T. Alfred Momo, Peter S. Dolo, Samuel B. Elliot, and Kaymore Kamara of the above tribes. Maybe, the spelling of the word "but" for each of the above tribes may vary but not the pronunciation and meaning. It's believed that few of the tribes that surround Bong County pronounce and interpret the word "but" as *kei/keh/geh*, thus indicating the exact origin. Other tribes in Liberia may pronounce "but," being translated as *geh or gei* by other Liberian tribes, which resembles the same tune or pronunciation with *keh/kei*. As you read on, break and ask some other Liberian tribes around you right now about the pronunciation and meaning of the word "but" before you continue. Just do this to investigate and authenticate what you have read.

The second evidence of the same historical origin among the Liberian tribes is the use and pronunciation of the words "*soore*," which means horse in English and, "*mena* or *miahn*," which means spoon by many Liberian tribes. A third reason to further validate the statement that most Liberian tribes hailed from the same origin is the practice of the Poro or Porlon fraternity for the men and the Sande for women, which further solidifies the proposition of the same origin because many tribes in Liberia are practicing them. Finally, if you survey some words used by many Liberian tribes, you get to understand that there are still many other words that are used, pronounced, and interpreted the same way, like BUT and SOORE.

Dear readers, you are encouraged to verify for yourselves what you read to enable you to help others with references.

Although the spelling for some words with similar meanings among these tribes may not be the same, you will realize that many Liberian tribes use them in the same context, meaning, and same pronunciation. Therefore, my assertion is based on the pronunciation and the meaning of these words mentioned above and not necessarily the spelling since they are African words.

The Kpelle ethnic group in current day Liberia is believed to have been among people who escaped to settle here. As such, this Kpelle tribe has been figured out among the rest of the tribes as a case study intended to educate our readers and incoming generations to practice and uphold the tradition and custom to avoid future brain-drain, which seems to be consequential and unavoidable if not addressed. This book is not capturing the customary practice of the Kpelle people before their arrival here in Liberia but rather the practices among them here on the land now called Liberia. It isn't easy to trace people from the first or second generation who migrated from Sudan to settle here. This is why we are working with key informants within the age range of 60 to 100 plus years old to feed us with trusted information because currently, you cannot find 150 years old person or above in our midst. If you are fortunate to see some more senior people in this age range, about 98% of them might not provide essential information due to limited knowledge. It is very difficult to see a member or members of the 13th-18th centuries' people and below still alive in our midst to provide information on customary marriage during their time from Sudan to what is now called Liberia.

Our work is based on the fact that the influence of western marriage is gradually engulfing our tradition and customary marriage procedures and the steps required for a complete ceremony to be held. The Kpelle tribe in Bong County is no exception from Western marriage's influence on customary marriage.

This significant influence over customary marriage procedures has triggered us to pen down this literature for all, even if you are not of the Kpelle tribe. This will remind you and me to know that something is going wrong and needs serious attention before it's too late. As part of my overview, the below analogy will help us better understand why things are going the way they are within our traditional marriage procedures.

Surprisingly, humankind's attitude is complicated and oblivious to comprehend as a human being is God, the Creator's, direct image or representative. Although, as the famous biblical quotation says in Genesis, "*Man was made in the image of God*," it is unbelievable to see us, humans, created by God with five senses and left with the options to decide our fate in terms of decision making to be involved with godlessness, lawlessness, stubbornness, and evils.

Homosexualism, lesbianism, concept of transgender, bestiality, wars, coup d'état, bloodshed, human trafficking, man-made viruses, corruption, greed for power, invention of weapons of mass destruction, arm robbery, disrespect of elders and traditions, human rights abuse, and many more have become standard practices as the order of our generation. Nonetheless, let me be clear that we are not compiling biblical tracts, nor preaching a sermon on the mount, but rather reminding us of our attitudes damaging our culture; a just cause visible enough to move us to write down what we are reading. I am also reminding us that the spirits of our ancestors are watching us with eagle eyes in the traditional realm and that doomsday lies right ahead of us in the soonest possible time for those who claim to be Christians/Muslim or God-fearing people.

Are we mindful that even members of the minor class of animals do not behave the way we sometimes do? If human-kind allows a male dog to have sex with a female human being, what do we think will be the byproduct? Why do we men cannot allow ourselves to have sex with a female dog? Why do men rape women, especially babies and teenagers? Do these acts form part of marriage? Women of the world, women of Liberia, and women of the Kpelle tribe, what do you think of us men, and how do you consider yourselves if you allow a dog as your sex mate under men's influence just for money or nothing? What are your values, then? Is it possible for a man who knows you as the girlfriend of dogs to marry you? Well, I will leave it just like this in suspense for everyone to answer conscientiously. But I think that everyone knows that a couple must love and kiss each other and maybe marry each other with happiness and pleasure in the end. But can these happen in such circumstances mentioned above? Will there be happiness or offspring out of such union between human versus dog? I guess, *NO*, as a response in capital letters.

We, as the first-class animal, as we term ourselves, some-times behave in a way that devalues our existence even below the attitude of the minor class of animals. This is because the dogs, chickens, cats, ants, goats, and animals of the wild do not practice or encourage the concept of same-sex marriage or mating. A male dog cannot mate with another male dog, or a male leopard cannot have sex with another male leopard or vise-versa. Similarly, as ugly as the baboon is, the behavior is not as ugly as human behaviors. The male baboon does not and will never mate with a same-sex baboon in any way because they are under the direct supervision and obedience of nature, if not God, from the day of creation to the present. Suppose this happens contrary to my above analogical thought. In that case, I will be convinced to conclude that it was manipulated by humankind because we are the engineers and crafters behind the good, the bad, and ugliest ideas. Bestiality has become the order of the day.

Of recent, it was reported on Radio Super Bongese in Gbarnga that a man believed to be in his early 20s has had intimacy with a female dog in Bong County, an incidence that has never occurred among us. Let me not deviate or divert your concentration from our main theme because I know that the ancestors are watching and that doomsday is awaiting you and me. The above analogy is made to correlate and showcase how far our missteps from customary marriage procedures and other traditional practices have carried us a long way from the original ones due to our creativity and innovations. For example, you cannot cut a man's head and replace it with the head of a woman, neither cut nor replace the head of a goat with a leopard to have the same class of animals still distinctly. This is impossible because it was not part of the designs of God's creation initially. These cruel acts and many more have seriously induced substantial negative implications on our customary marriages, which need serious attention.

The next chapter will elaborate on the influence and consequences of western marriage on customary marriage as the results of our attitudes and behaviors discussed in chapter two above.

Chapter Three

Influence and Consequences of Western Marriage on Customary Marriage in Liberia

Western influence in every capacity across the world, including our culture, has dramatically changed things from old fashion to new, including Liberia and Bong County. It is no secret that the biblical and social western influence on Liberia and our customary marriage is enormous. This requires serious attention; otherwise, our culture and tradition will surely wear away and might indeed be replaced with western ideology or a new breed of culture altogether.

We will try hard not to be xenophobic in our deliberations but rather articulate factual information that you can rely on. My argument is not based on racial discrimination as others may think. But as things unfold, you will also see our faults as African people and Liberians, including the Kpelle tribe. Our "see and copy from everywhere attitudes," our negligence and don't-care-attitudes to learn, practice, and uphold the tradition from our people (the elderly) who lived before us, are also some of the push factors responsible for the missing links within our customary marriage procedures.

For many centuries ago, our great-great-grandparents and fore-parents lived and married through customary means only. Everything concerning traditional marriage was done one hundred percent exclusive of western influence. Only the Conquered-elite (Americo-Liberians) class married the western way during the founding stages of the land now called Liberia. Traditionally, the bride was usually engaged to a groom unknowingly until they reached maturity, where they are joined together as husband and wife. This ceremony was purely customary marriage and was always conducted by the parents, guardians, family members, and close relatives. The ceremony was purely conducted customarily through traditional rites. A traditional package was usually prepared for the bride by her parents and presented to her in the presence of the groom and his family as a symbol of farewell and empowerment. Inside the package included basic things like a cook-spoon (wooden, silver, or gold), mortar, fanner, clean or unbeaten rice, and basic home utensils like pot, dishes, knife, seeds, etc. This was done to avoid the husband from boasting over the bride while in the married home because some men most often say to the woman, *"What did you bring here into this home? Nothing."*

Gowning the parents and other close relatives of the bride has always been an integral part of this ceremony. Traditional music and dances usually accompanied the occasion for entertainment. There was nothing called "check or search for your bride" or an engagement ring at the ceremony with extra financial attachment. The provision of kola nuts, $48.00USD, coin (10 cents, 50 cents, one dollar, etc.), breakable plates, and sometimes cattle played a significant part during the customary marriage. The tusk of an elephant, leopard tooth, eagle wing, silver, and other valuable and hard-to-find items was sometimes used to marry a bride. According to traditional experts, these items are the central focus or ingredients for the customary marriage. Without them, there was no successful customary marriage. The driving away of muus (uncle, nephew, or family members who claim to be the owners of the bride) has been a very significant part of the ceremony even up to the present day. *Muu,* in the Jorquelleh Kpelle tribe, is someone from the bride's family who traditionally claims to be the owner or husband of the bride being married. The *muu* or *muus* will do everything possible traditionally to embarrass the ongoing ceremony unless he is driven away satisfactorily with some tokens in line with the custom. Extra taxation levied on the groom's family has never been part of the customary marriage from the old days. There has only been one bride prepared for the groom on this occasion and not two, three, four, five, or more brides as seen in modern days. A woman or bride was never married in just one day or within a shorter time. In the old days, the search for a bride was done with patience for quite a long time with keen observation. The parents of a groom-to-be were never responsible for serving as hosts for the traditional marriage ceremony.

The acronym "LOVE" was seriously taken into consideration during the search for a bride. The "L" in love represents Look, the "O" stands for Observe, the "V" is for Venture, and the "E" is to Engage. Before you could take the hand of a bride in the days of old, you must look carefully, observe keenly, venture into it appropriately and then engage the woman you wanted traditionally.

But the introduction of western marriage ideology coupled with our weak attitudes has encouraged deviation from the culture, including double-marriage, which has become the order of the day. Double-marriage means a couple who has undergone a successful traditional or customary marriage and yet went ahead to conduct a western marriage or vise versa. There are several reasons for double-marriage in our setting today. First, this is because the customary marriage initially did not provide modern documentation like a certificate or license to guarantee the relationship legally in ancient times. It was only later the idea of a tribal certificate came into the picture. A second reason is that the traditional marriage gives rise to the man or husband in the home to marry more than one wife, which the church and modern wife will never accept. A third reason is that modern man wants to prove himself, compete with others in life, and live a life that will commensurate his status and even beyond.

But as time goes by, the stages of man have gradually improved from primitive to modern man. The changes in the stages of man have brought vast negative transformation to customary marriage in terms of practice and procedures. Modern Liberian man has divided western matrimony into two categories called African wedding and western wedding. In this case, the only difference you might see between the two is the dress code, while the foodstuffs, the agenda, and drinks are sometimes the same or mixed. In most instances, the music played at the ceremony is both African and Western. Every other activity seems to be intertwined or similar, including the procedures and dances. And so the questions are, where are we heading? What is the difference between the two types of marriages (customary & western marriages)? Can we uphold and maintain our culture and tradition if we continue like this? Each of us can answer these questions for ourselves and design measures to mitigate these problems, undermining the procedures of customary marriage.

Since I have embarked on this journey as a social scientist, it is incumbent on me to inform you that incorporating these western practices into our customary marriages seriously undermines and damages our marriage procedures as a byproduct. And if we continue, all the prescribed steps and practices will get lost, and we will be putting the first step in the place of the second step, the second step in the place of step five, or bring the last step first and then the first shall be the last. This will be a mockery of our tradition if we cannot uphold the right or correct practices that our forefathers started and practiced. This is one reason why we have hospitals in Liberia, and top government officials still seek medical attention in the diaspora, even if it is a malaria case. This is a mockery of our health system. And if this continues, our health facilities will be as useless as the sputum of cough.

Let me give you another practical example of the misapplication of our marriage procedures; I was told by one of our many contributors that he went to dowry a bride and was asked to make the dowry payment before the gowning ceremony. What a shame on the custom; see how ridiculous it is. How can you dowry the bride before conducting the gowning exercise, which should come before the dowry payment? Where did such practice come from? I called this "disrespect before the due respect" in that you cannot marry your woman first before honoring her parents.

Dear readers, I want you to remember that this is part of the evidence that western ideology has taken a considerable lead over customary marriage. And so, do not be complacent or sycophantic with the few justifications provided here by me; check for more facts to convince yourselves on how foreign practices have influenced your culture. Dowry payment before gowning the parents means taking possession of the bride before giving due respect to her parents, your in-laws. I'm afraid that's not right and must be abolished. We must gown the parents first to provide them with the honor and happiness to pave the way for the dowry payment.

The gowning is the highest honor for the biological parents of the bride on this occasion, so you cannot take the daughter of a family into your possession before giving them back this respect. How can you possess the bride and then want to dowry her again? To whom are you paying the dowry when she is already in your possession? Remember that the tradition demands that dowry payment be made first before possessing the bride and not possession before dowry payment. This is similar to what modern men are doing. They can first jump into the girlfriend and boyfriend relationship and even produce a child or children before marriage. In this way, the pregnancy is turned over to the boy's or man's family from the very beginning. Then, after living together and producing several children, they decide to get married without officially returning the woman to her parents in line with the tradition. This means that the woman is already in your possession and wants to marry her. How can you marry a woman or bride from yourself? By interpretation, you are serving as the parents and the groom at the same. This was not and should never be part of our traditional practices in line with customary marriage.

Let me bring to our attention that most of these additions and subtractions within the customary marriage procedures are happening because modern men are fighting to raise more money and prove that their ceremony was the best and most organized one among the rest. This is one reason why about two or more fake or counterfeit ladies are prepared in the name of the main bride to be wedded so that the groom and his family can patiently search for their bride among them one at a time until she is found. This process requires money. Every step taken, and every single lappa taken down from each of these ladies, is paid for until all the ladies are brought forward before the original bride can appear. In addition to the above, a special charge is sometimes imposed on the groom's family to pay apart from the $48USD.

Moreover, to raise more money during this ceremony, the women escorting the fake brides and the main bride will intentionally stop or slow down and complaint that the vehicle or airplane bringing each of the brides has either broken down and needs fuel, gasoline, repair, medical treatment for the driver, and so on. The only remedy to these multiple problems mentioned above is to pay money to rescue the situation to enable each of the so-called brides to appear at the unveiling ceremony. The motive behind these countless requests is to raise funds from the exercise, which is often boring and irritating. The idea of the modern search for the bride is most often introduced into the customary marriage ceremony by the friends and some family members of the bride. However, the majority of the grooms do not support the concept of searching for the bride in the modern way.

These are just part of the influences our customary marriage is undergoing that are breaking the culture and tradition apart to the extent that the center can no longer hold. It is forbidden for the groom to perform his own traditional marriage ceremony. Your father or uncle or a proxy must represent and spearhead all ceremony activities as you take the hand of your bride. Your role and satisfaction are to receive your bride's hand at the end of the entire ceremony. But some modern-day grooms are now conducting and spearheading their own traditional marriage ceremony, which is not advisable. A groom should not be very active during this ceremony. In fact, it was sometimes difficult to easily and quickly notice the groom's presence at the wedding except maybe by the dress code or through introduction or close interactions.

To enlighten our minds and help us uphold our Kpelle ethnic group's customary marriage procedures for this and incoming generations, the following chapter has been well articulated and well-tailored for our readers, the users, and would-be teachers. The steps and procedures required for customary marriage will help our readers, the adults, the youths, and the incoming generations to understand and perform customary marriages independently, which will live with us till death do us part as the couple usually says.

Chapter Four

The Basic Steps and Procedures Required for Customary Marriage

A Guide to Customary Marriage is written to help us understand and maintain our lost dignity, tradition, culture, and custom, especially to traditional marriage among the 16 Liberian ethnic groups, emphasizing the Jorquelleh Kpelle of the Kpelle tribe. As previously mentioned in our introduction, the focus of this literature is squarely placed on the steps and procedures that are traditionally prescribed and required to marry a woman through customary means in the Jorquelleh Kpelle people fashion or setting in Bong County. This part of our literary work puts the Jorquelleh Kpelle people's way of customary marriage under the spotlight, which our great-great-grandparents and ancestors started many centuries ago. We will try to trace some of what has happened among our people when taking a bride's hand as our area of concern.

The focus of this chapter is not about what is currently happening now where the western marriage procedures and other factors have already greatly influenced the customary marriage over time. However, some current customary steps and procedures will be considered for our use because some were initially used by the early people who started this ceremony. Some of the modern practices of our customary marriage are deeply inculcated into this manuscript for learning purposes and not to use them for our custom. The inclusion of some current practices is also meant to help us understand the difference between what is happening today as customary marriage practice and what has been prescribed and practiced by our forefathers. Comparing the current and past practices of customary marriage procedures are injected to separate and to know the best customary practices from the proliferated practices. We are advised in this chapter to learn both practices (old & new) and only practice and sustain the original prescribed and required practices for customary marriage as our focus. These good or best practices in the text are highlighted or emphasized through instructions to help you identify the preferable ones from those not considered part of the practice.

According to Mr. Mulbah T. Jacob, my late father, Ma Gorli-kawuan, and our many contributors to this book, boys and girls did not have the slightest idea of saying that I want you as my fiancé in the days of old. They did not mention what we call boyfriend or girlfriend today. About one or less century ago, boys or mature men for marriage did not say to a girl "I want to marry you" directly. If a girl was approached by a boy or a man for marriage, she never agrees all by herself unless she consults her mother. The mother then consults her husband because the parents knew precisely the background of that fellow proposing. If the parents did not know the groom's background, it was incumbent upon them to do their background investigation before responding. This background check was easy to do because the marriage was highly endogamous. This wasn't a matter of one day, week, or one month, but it required time. LOVE, as an acronym, was used to look, observe, venture, and then engage whosoever was the target of the groom and family.

Parents did not allow their children to marry from bad-mannered families or families with problematic backgrounds. The parents of the brides-to-be most often rejected grooms from troublesome backgrounds. In fact, in many instances, when a girl child was born into another home, the first parents to engage the child through her parents for their son may likely be the one to marry that boy, depending on the family's characters. Sometimes when a woman was impregnated, and the belly is visible, another man or family will pre-engage it through the husband of the *big-belly* (Pregnant woman) so that if the child is a girl, she will become a daughter-in-law or a wife to a son from the family who did the earliest pre-engagement.

The background, as mentioned above, has a broader and deeper traditional interpretation. The background has to do with the characters of both partners who want to form a union. These characters include traditional norms, cultures, diet or types of food eaten, dress code, individual or family track record, fraternity or type of society practiced, religious affiliation, and even life before and after marriage. In addition, support to both parents after marriage between their children was a vital component of the background investigation. This means that each party involved in coming together to build this future relationship must meticulously investigate or verify those critical areas of their lives style and accept the culture of each other vise-versa. If you fail to verify each other's background, you might surely suffer the consequences in the end.

Let me be a bit practical here by giving one or two examples of the diet or food eaten and the type of society your husband-to-be or wife-to-be associates themselves with before you can venture into marriage. In the first place, if you do not find out the type of food your fiancé and family do eat before marriage, you might undoubtedly end up eating human meat, scorpion, *zoglo*, dog, your taboo, or the unthinkable food before you can come to your senses. Do not allow yourself to reach a point where you will say, "I never knew or had I known." This is a serious regret without a defined solution.

For example, a pastor was invited to preach during an African wedding ceremony in a church (unnamed) in Ganta. According to one of our many contributors (Mr. Peter S. Dolo), the pastor began with a song in Mano which says, *"nehn-leh leh zoglo, zoglo leh nehn-nehn."* By interpretation, the song means a small child can't eat *zoglo*; *zoglo* is very sweet. *Zoglo* is a particular caterpillar eaten by some tribes in eastern Nimba County, close to the Liberian-Ivorian border. Probably, I have eaten some of this in a meal unknowingly because I lived in Nimba for four consecutive years and ate almost all the Nimbaian foods during my stay.

The sermon's theme was "Assessing and Accepting the Culture of Your Partner Before Venturing into Marriage." After the song, the pastor narrated a short story in real life that a groom married his bride on one beautiful Saturday in Ganta, Nimba County. The wedding was very colorful and successful. But few days after the ceremony, the newly wedded wife cooked a delicious meal (GB) for her newly wedded husband, which contained *zoglo*. After eating the soup, the newly married man asked his wife about the mixtures or ingredients of the delicious soup. When the wife explained to him that it was the *zoglo* (caterpillar) that made the soup so delicious, he also asked what *zoglo* is because the name of this thing was foreign or strange to him. In response, she told him that *zoglo* is a caterpillar widely eaten by her tribe. Upon receiving this information and glancing at this creature (*zoglo*), he got very annoyed. He threatened to disengage the newly established marital relationship due to the lack of communication before preparing the meal with the husband's type of food (forbidden). This is a delicious mess, he said. He became furious. How can you cook caterpillars for me, my so-called wife, he asked?

And this became a serious problem in their home because the man failed to find out about his wife's background before marriage. Finally, the marriage deepened into confusion and broke apart and could not hold because of their incompatibility based on food consumption. This was further compounded by the increase in the dividers within their home. Moreover, the marriage was exogamous in that he hailed from another tribe with different backgrounds and attitudes in totality. Had he found out the types of food this woman and her family eat in addition to GB, he would never marry this bride with pride. GB is the most common name of a popular food among Nimbaians (Mano & Gio tribes). It is usually prepared from cassava tuber with a slippery soup most often dominated by dry meat and *zoglo* itself sometimes.

A newly wedded wife disengaged from her short-lived matrimonial partnership in a second related story because her husband was involved with a secret society that deals with human sacrifice for riches. Her husband's riches fooled her. As such, she failed to dig deeper into his characters before making her final decision about marriage. After their marriage, several rumors came about her husband that he was a ritualistic killer. She did not care to verify the stories surrounding the alleged ritualistic attitudes of the man. Some family members informed her about the rumors that were mongering around them concerning her husband's involvement. She did not trust the news sources, neither did she try to find out before marriage. But she later observed her husband was always out during night hours up to 3 or 4 AM most often.

She finally decided to test the water. Fortunately and unfortunately for her, she automatically divorced her husband because it did not take a long time when she caught her husband right-handed after destroying the life of another person just for money. This happened when she fooled the husband and said that she was traveling somewhere for a week. She returned two days later ahead of the planned schedule around midnight and hid around their compound. Her husband arrived and came down from the vehicle so bloody up. The Ghana-Must-Go bag was in his hands with droplets of blood. She sneaked out to get people (her brothers) she had previously contacted, and they came immediately and caught the man right handy. There was no room for denial or escape for this newly married man during this incident, and as such, his wife was emotionally forced to make a decision that was not pre-planned.

But the questions are, was this decision timely? Was it her plan to disengage the relationship so soon like this? I guess no, as the only answer to these questions because you already learned that she accepted the proposal for marriage and the man's culture without background investigation. It was too late for her to investigate the background of the man. The best time to investigate the background of your partner-to-be is before marriage, be it traditional or statutory. *Do not mind the grease of the meat and take it from the fire hearth with your tongue.* (a parable from my late father)

Beware that all fathers are men, but not all men are fathers. Similarly, all husbands are men, but not all men are the husbands you expect. Not all that glitters is gold, but all gold surely glitters, though.

Similarly, in connection to the stories above, many married couples have relinquished their marital relationships because either one or both members of the partnership did not care to dig out information about life before and after marriage. Many Liberian parents feel that their daughter or son must continue to provide support of all kinds as a return benefit for the child's upbringing even after marriage. Failure on the part of one of the newly married couple to comply in helping the husband's or the wife's parents, conflict is inevitable in this home. Conflict may come and may even lead to separation or divorce simply because one of them does not agree that they give financial or material support to either one of their parents. Please check out and dig deeper behind your partner-to-be to identify those attitudes that are not compatible with yours before making a final decision to marry, be it customary or western marriage.

These two real-life stories (nonfictional), as narrated above, ended up in divorce because the victims in both cases did not check the characters of their partners before marriage. You are advised not to behave like these victims, or else the consequences will surely hunt you and destroy your relationship, your honey (love), and your money forever.

As a reconnect, when two men were best friends in the community or village, either of the two could tell his colleague that if his wife gets impregnated and the baby is a girl child, then I will give her to you as a wife for your son. Upon giving birth and establishing that the child is a female, a message was sent quickly to the friend or family that was previously promised to appear on the scene to see their wife-to-be immediately. If the previously promised man was suitable to receive the message from another person or a different source, he was obligated to move in to pre-engage the child officially quickly. As a tradition, white color beads were tied on the child's wrist, or a silver banger was put on the wrist as a mark of identity for the initial engagement. This mark indicates that this girl child has been pre-engaged by someone and that there is no space or vacancy for anyone to venture again. Sometimes kola nuts and other valuable items like silver were used for this pre-engagement exercise.

In simple words, the parents were those responsible for looking for a bride for their son to marry. At that time, I dare you (girl or boy) to say *no* to that decision approved by both parents. That person automatically becomes your lifetime partner whether you like it or not. This is precisely what happened in the case of my late mother, Ma Gorpu. Her big brother, Mulbah T. Jacob, told me that she was initially pre-engaged by another family for their son when she was a little girl. She was then taken into that home innocently to go through training from the second parents with the intent to help that girl child and her family based on her parents' vulnerability. As a result, she grew up in her future husband's home without knowing each other in bed until they reached the age of maturity. Before her age of maturity, she did not even know the main purpose of being in that home. At this point upon maturity, my parents-to-be were then traditionally joined together as husband and wife. And her marital relationship lasted with my father till their untimely demise.

Unlike these days where we younger ones look for our own woman or man, this was not the case in the old days with our forefathers. The two children were considered as couple-in-waiting unknowingly until they reach the required age range at that time (maturity). Their parents determined the time for them to marry, who had their criteria for that ceremony. They did not know what we call age today. Parents determined age based on the number of different rice farms they have cultivated over time. The child's mother was responsible for monitoring and determined the maturity of her child for marriage. At the age of marriage (maturity), both parents arranged a schedule, at which time they will conduct that special ceremony for customary marriage for their children. We were told that maturity was sometimes determined by the fall of the breasts or tay-tay of the girl.

There is no doubt that the groom's family always went away to the bride's home or the girl's family because they are the ones looking for something in that home. As the Liberian adage goes, *"He who has interest or property across the river will always have his trousers wet."* And so, *"If you visit the home of the bats, you just have to hang like a bat."* And if you visit the home of the fish, you will have to swim like a fish to survive and succeed. This aspect of the tradition (conducting the ceremony at the home of the bride & parents) is still being widely respected and used. Though a minute spectrum of the society sometimes tries to hijack or influence the ceremony to be conducted at the groom's home, the best practice, as we were told, is to have the wedding ceremony done at the home of the bride's parents. How can you control another person's home as a visitor?

This is one of our major mistakes that are causing missteps and conflicts within our customary marriages. The formula for both western and traditional marriages is that the man, commonly known as the groom, must go away to another home to take his bride's hand and bring her to his home. Genesis 2:24 vividly affirms this tradition that the man must leave his father and mother to unite with his wife. Traditional experts have advised us men (grooms) not to marry the woman at our home because it devalues her womanhood and shows gross disrespect to her parents, in any case, be it customary or statutory marriage. Even if you have built a new house and plan to host the ceremony at your old home as a groom and intend to take your newly wedded wife in the new home, please do not host the ceremony at your home; it lacks respect and moral. It promotes disadvantage over the bride and her parents.

Let the bride's parents host you, and the ceremony as the tradition dictates. The customary marriage process requires different stages, steps, and procedures that cannot permit anyone to marry his bride in one day or in a shorter time.

On this occasion, an introduction from both sides of the bride and groom is made, followed by welcome remarks from the bride's family. This is because the groom and family members were always and will always be the guests of honor. After this, space is provided by the host for the groom's family to make their case heard. It is the perfect opportunity through which the groom's father or representative gives the purpose of their visit, including the official declaration of intent. At this point, the ceremonial ball gets rolling for business. I want you to please understand that the couple-in-waiting up to this time does not necessarily need to know each other before the day of marriage. It was never a matter of compulsion. They were not rapacious for sex before marriage. Their dating was controlled or done by their parents. The restrictions were very titanic, strict, unbending, rigid, and respected. There was no bypass to the process by the boy, neither the girl who was very committed. The master of the ceremony comes typically from the family of the bride and not from the groom. They are the ones in charge of the program from start to end. The groom and family are advised not to take control of the ceremony; otherwise, you will be bending and crippling our dear custom. Please play the roles and responsibilities that your in-laws and the tradition required of you at that ceremony as you gear up to take the hand of your bride.

The formalities outlined below here have been carefully verified to help you and future generations to learn, practice, and uphold our customary marriage practices and procedures in uniformity. You may call it agenda.

Summary of basic steps & procedures prescribed to marry a Jorquelleh Kpelle woman

According to our key informants and many contributors, the entire processes and procedures for the customary ceremony typically include the following;

1. Self-introduction
2. Welcome remarks
3. Inquiry of why you are here
4. Declaration of intent/expression of interest
5. A period of questions and answers
6. Searching for the bride
7. Engagement of the bride
8. Driving away the *Muus*
9. The dowry payment
10. Presentation of the bride to the groom's family

11. Presentation of the bride's farewell package
12. Vote of thanks and closing remarks
13. Entertainment (eating, singing, dancing & drinking.)

According to our key informants, the above-listed items are the basic summary of the required protocol for a customary marriage ceremony among the Jorquelleh Kpelle tribe in Liberia. Despite the adjustment and modifications made by modern people, we know this as a practice so far from our interviewees.

Details of the prescribed basic steps and procedures or protocols at the ceremony

The entire ceremony begins with the introduction of major participants or key players when everyone is well seated. During the introduction, members of both families will call their names and positions or functions within their respective families. This can be done individually or through a representative from each side.

The introduction is followed by a welcome remark from the bride's family as the host. The welcome remark usually precedes a segment which is the period of inquiries from the bride's family. First, the family head of the bride must ask the visitors for the purpose of their visit. Why are you here is usually asked, and then the floor is given to the groom's family for the response. The father or uncle or an approved representative of the groom will then come up to speak.

The Declaration of Intent

The declaration of intent begins with the groom's family upon the invitation from their in-laws. At this point, the groom's father, or representative, takes the stage and explains that they have come to take the hand of a girl they have seen in this home as a wife for their son. Then, in line with the tradition, a token called *ku-woe-kao* is given to the bride's family. *Ku-woe-kao* in the Kpelle tribe is like a white kola or money presented to validate what someone has said to guarantee their statement. This is proof or evidence of the official statement that the groom's family has made. It can be a white kola nut, money, or any valuable item with greater value or respect. *Ku-woe-kao* is the evidence of the statement made to solidify their claims that they are here for that purpose.

Questions and answers period

After the declaration of intent, several questions are most often asked. These questions come from the bride's family to the visitors. Key questions usually asked among many include the following;

1. What is the name of the woman whom you are talking about?
2. Who will be our father-in-law for this ceremony?
3. Who will be our mother-in-law?
4. Who asked you or begged you to come to marry our daughter?
5. Where are you taking our daughter after marriage?
6. Do you see any marks or bruises on her body?
7. Are you able to take good care of our child?

The above questions are some of the many questions always asked and answered before the ceremony can proceed, as they are very cardinal to the process. Question number 6 above is most often asked right after giving the bride's hand to the groom and family. This segment is what we called the questions and answers period at the traditional marriage ceremony.

Searching for the Bride

Searching for the bride is another formality at the ceremony, allowing modern people to dress two, three, or more false brides besides the main bride to fool the visitors and raise money. These extra ladies are well-attired and again covered with more pieces of lappa or wider cloths so that no one can easily identify them until they are unveiled. They are all kept in a secret place, sometimes in the house, so that no one sees them unless the protocols are observed. These counterfeit brides are prepared in the name of the main bride to be wedded so that the groom and his family can patiently search for their bride among them until she is found. This process requires money; every step taken and every single lappa removed from each of these ladies is paid for until all the ladies are brought forward and unveiled, one at a time, before the original bride can appear at last.

This was not the case with the original custom. According to our key informants, the search was practiced by people who started the ceremony, but no money or fees were paid. The search was based on the groom's or the bride's family background. This was done to avoid sending your girl or boy child to the wrong or worst family to marriage. The visitors were asked to identify the woman or bride among the rest of the women in that home free of charge. It was intended to identify the bride in question by calling her name and pointing at her openly during the marriage ceremony and not in secret. This was mainly done for the rest of the people who did not know the bride to be known to the public, the kind of search our forefathers were involved in instead of the modern-day search for the bride.

Moreover, in the modern era, to raise more money during this ceremony, the women escorting the fake brides and the main bride will intentionally complaint that the vehicle or airplane bringing each of the brides has either broken down, needs fuel, gasoline, repair, medical treatment for the driver or the bride, and so on. These requests are repeated throughout the process for each of the brides, whether the main one or the fake brides. The only remedy to these problems mentioned above is to pay money to rescue the situation to enable each of the so-called brides to appear at the ceremony to be unveiled.

The motive behind these countless requests is designed to raise funds from the exercise, which is often boring and irritating. In fact, those who play the groom's role or serves as the groom do not know the suffering that these brides, including the main bride, undergo at the ceremony, especially during the heat of the dry season. Someone said that *"heat makes cow liver done,"* and so parents and friends, are you causing too much or prolong heat to suffer your own bride whom you have entangled with the actual wedding attire plus extra pieces of lappa or cloth? What is her happiness then, and where is your love toward her?

My keen observations show that monies raised at such a ceremony are not often reported to the bride's parents but are instead shared among friends and followers of the bride who grouped themselves for that purpose. And yet, the parents of the bride are always in support of this modern-day search for the bride. In fact, in most instances, the bride does not know how much fund is raised by her colleagues from her wedding ceremony unless she sometimes asks a few days, weeks, or months later.

My dear female friends to the bride, please stop the prolonged practice of searching for the bride. The heat can embarrass the bride that even you cannot withstand, especially during the dry season. If you want to know the weight of the cat, you turn into a rat. Parading three or more fake brides before the arrival of the main bride in the name of raising money is for your gain at the detriment of the bride. This is not a good practice for our beloved culture. It is very uncomfortable, humiliating, and even suffocative. We, therefore, discourage you, please abandon your quest for the modern-day search of the bride. This is also time-consuming, as you may be aware. Let me be a bit contradictory by encouraging you to, at least, parade one or two fake brides to satisfy your desire instead of more brides to avoid the punishment on the bride.

According to our respondents, all monies and cattle collected at such ceremonies in the old days were solely controlled and used by the bride's family and not the followers or agents of the bride or the groom.

It was even forbidden for unmarried women or girls to play a significant role at this ceremony because they are blind and lack the experience to proceed. Uninvited guests did not meddle in the exercise unless you are requested to perform a given task. The traditions forbid an unmarried person to lead somebody getting married because they are not a member of the marital society and do not have the technical know-how. How can the blind lead the blinds? If this happens, they will surely fall together into the pit. Our old customary marriage tradition does not allow non-member of the left-hand society (married people) to lead or overshadow the ceremony.

Still, when one of the false brides is unveiled in search of the bride, she is led by this group of women (self-organized) to sit on a special mat prepared for them. It is the responsibility of the groom or his family to spread this mat or pay for the services leading to the spreading of this traditional mat. When they all have appeared one by one and unveiled, the main bride is then escorted by this special organized group of women in the same manner and form. The women usually include family members, relatives, and friends of the bride. The bride will also sit on the same mat after her unveiling exercise is completed.

Before starting the engagement rite, there is a final request from these women that the visitors must address: to pay the transportation fare for each of the duplicate brides to go back home so that the main bride can have a free and spacious environment to sit. Again, readers, this requires money from the visitors before the process can continue.

Dear readers, we want to categorically let you understand that this was never in the case of our forefathers and is therefore not counted as part of the tradition. Furthermore, this modern-day search for the bride has never been a key factor or practice anywhere within the customary marriage ceremony. As such, traditional experts have advised us not to follow suit.

In my view, apart from generating money from the unveiling exercise, this is probably done to add beauty to the occasion. If you think you cannot conduct your traditional marriage ceremony without the modern-day search for the bride, please be moderate. Do not suffer the bride in the heat for so long until her happiness turns into pain, agony, or frustration. Please try to parade for me at least one or two counterfeit brides before the main bride can surface. It will help reduce her punishment as a bride since you cannot do your traditional marriage without it. When the fake brides are sent home in the modern customary marriage after the unveiling exercise, the doors to the engagement exercise are then opened for business. In my view, addition to the customary marriage procedures in good fate may not be a bad thing. Still, the subtraction of some of the original practices from the custom might be the worst thing ever to do against our tradition.

The engagement Exercise

The engagement is the official way of showing yourself and letting the bride's family know that this is the woman you want. For this reason, the bride's family should not allow any other man to apply for the vacancy for their daughter. You have come to engage their daughter and get back home to prepare yourself to marry her traditionally. In this case, both parents of the groom-to-be and the bride-to-be are officially informed and aware of the relationship. This will oblige them to be watchdogs and advisers to both parties.

At this point (the engagement), the groom's family has prepared a breakable plate with the engagement and kola nuts inside it. Please remember that this plate (first plate) is not returnable though modern humans return it to be re-used for the dowry payment. This is wrong and lacks respect according to the tradition. It shows the groom's unpreparedness, ignorance, stinginess, and weakness of the groom and family. The plate, kola nuts, and coin make up the engagement package. And so, you cannot give away respect and then take it back with the anticipation to resend. This is naïve and unspeakable beyond all imagination in our traditional realm. I witnessed this when I independently conducted a customary marriage ceremony for my niece in Gbarnga in 2020. The groom and his family were all novices to the procedures; they begged us to return the engagement plate given to us during the program, which we did under a reluctant condition to avoid disgrace and delay.

My beloved readers, this doesn't seem right and is unacceptable; and is therefore not advisable to emulate. Please prepare and take with you two separate breakable and high valuable plates for your traditional marriage program, one for the engagement and the other for the dowry payment. Because we did it does not mean that it is correct and accepted by the tradition. Let me admit that we did this under a reluctant and difficult condition, and experts later advised us through consultations not to repeat such practice if we intend to improve and maintain the procedures.

Olden days engagement and dowry payment were done separately and not on the same day of dowry payment. This has been changed by us modern people; everything is done on the same day. The engagement has always been the first thing done alone on a separate day. Then the dowry payment exercise followed, sometimes weeks, months, or years later after the engagement ceremony has taken place. But today, however, modern people say that it is a waste of time to separate the two, which is why we do everything into one in this contemporary era. Some couples will choose to do the engagement one day, a week, or one month, or one year before the dowry payment schedule is made. Again, others will choose to conduct the engagement exercise together with the dowry payment on the same day instead of how it was done in the past.

Experts on traditional matters have advised us not to blend the two distinct components of our customary marriage.

Instead, they should create a space like days, weeks, months, or years in between to respect and maintain the custom. Combining everything into one day will cause you to leave out or skip some crucial things considering the many different steps, stages, and procedures involved. This is why our modern-day customary and western marriages can be long, boring, and uncomfortable to witness.

I remember my niece and her groom combining both traditional and western weddings on the same day. In their case, it/he was three into one because he still had our daughter in his possession when he impregnated her, and we turned her over to them. He possessed our daughter until they begat four children. I compelled him to turn her over during the morning hour of the same wedding day because I had some ideas on the tradition. This was hell-crazy, my people. It was unbearable though they succeeded under the harsh conditions because they did not listen to my advice and other people's advice far ahead of their ceremony. So don't be like them, or be prepared for pressure and maybe an incomplete or half-done ceremony.

This couple planned to start the traditional marriage by 9 AM. But instead, we began by 11:30 AM through 2:30 PM. Our daughter's forceful turnover or return to us was done around 10:00 AM before the traditional marriage could start. Based on these tight and ugly schedules, the western wedding started at 3:30 PM. I know most of you readers have some experience concerning the time interval for such a modern program. As a direct adverse effect, the western wedding ended around 7:00 PM, a time that some participants had already gone home because it was late, boring, and irritating.

In the continuity of the engagement exercise, the groom's father will now call on the groom's mother, the custodian of this package, to inspect and take the plate to the bride. The tradition also permits the mother or aunty (mother & sister to the groom's mother) to play the role of the mother. The uncle or father will then instruct the groom's mother to walk majestically to the mat where the bride is seated. She will then kneel down and respectfully present the engagement package to the bride for onward presentation to her parents, beginning with her mother.

We are told that the mother or aunt of the groom or a proxy can also present the token to the bride as a female proxy only. The bride will then walk and kneel before her mother and present the token or engagement in the plate to her mother, who then asks the bride for a response to the token given her and onward to other family members and then to the father at last.

The bride's mother usually asks her daughter, *"What do you say to the proposal from these visitors? The people say that they want to marry you as a wife to their son."*

She aims to understand whether or not the bride herself will willingly accept the proposal made. At this point, you have to hear from the horse's mouth for future reference. This means that it is a matter of compulsion for the bride to respond in the modern era.

In the days of old, the bride's grandmother, aunty, or the female family head was the one to give a response to the engagement plate. Any response from such family member was final, whether rejection or acceptance of the engagement. About 99% of the answer to *"The people say that they want you as a wife to their son"* is stated in this manner, *"Yes, Mother, I agree, and I do accept the proposal."*

There is always a shout of joy from the audience in celebration as soon as the proposal is endorsed. In some instances in the days of old, the bride's grandmother was the one to respond to the acceptance of the engagement on her daughter's behalf, and this was a final decision according to the tradition.

But modern-days brides in the Kpelle tradition are being permitted to speak openly because of the many laws on the book. These laws create the avenue for everyone above 18 years of age to decide for themselves. This is why a bride must respond to the engagement plate from the groom's family though this aspect was also scarcely practiced at that time.

Again, readers, I witnessed one traditional marriage program where there was no engagement and engagement plate at all. Instead, they immediately began the ceremony with the dowry payment. Then, the groom's family placed some kola nuts on a plate and presented it to the bride's family. They then received and accepted it and passed it on to the audience for pick and eat. This means that the groom's family welcomed the bride's family and the rest of the people though the bride's family hosted the ceremony. As far as we are concerned, this pattern was wrong and must not be imitated. This happened because those involved were not knowledgeable about the tradition.

There is a chain of family members through which the token passes before reaching the father. It starts with the bride's mother, who is already in possession of the engagement and will then get it to her close female family members like sisters, aunties, mother, grandmother, etc., for their blessings. The bride's mother then presents it to her husband (the bride's father) after the courtesy consultations with the special categories of women mentioned above. The bride's father will then return the token to his wife (the bride's mother) upon his approval to hold on yet as the process continues.

What the bride's father says typically is, *"We are very happy that our daughter has accepted the proposal, and so, I do now accept and endorse her 'will' on behalf of my family."*

This breakable plate contains some kola nuts and a coin as a token which is the backbone of the engagement. According to the traditionalists, this coin (could be 5 cents, 10 cents, 20 cents, 25 cents, 50 cents, or 1 dollar) is considered the token for the main engagement. The typical Kpelle name for the engagement token is *Welli-kao* (bone of engagement for the love/friendship). *Welli* in Kpelle means love, while *Kao* means bone. And so, the engagement token is the bone or backbone of the love by interpretation.

This is different from *Korli-kao*, the Jorquelleh Kpelle name for the dowry (the $48USD). *Korli-kao* means the bone of solemnization. In Kpelle, *Korli* means "to look for or marry," while *kao* means "bone or backbone." And so, this coin in the engagement is considered the token, strength, value, and backbone of the search and selection made for the bride.

Shilleng-tornor (20 cents) was sometimes used for engagement in the days of old. Shilleng derived from the British word "shilling" (British currency). It was earlier introduced into Liberia and used by our forefathers during the colonial period.

Pum-tornor (4 dollars/or 4 British pounds) was most common and sometimes used during such occasions. The official acceptance remark of the token from the bride's family concludes the entire engagement segment of the customary marriage procedures. Now that you have graduated from this level, part one of the traditional marriage procedures, your next focus is the dowry payment exercises, the second and final phase.

Driving the muus away

Before the dowry payment is made, you have to drive the *muus* away, always there to protest. The muu or *muus* are those male family members who claim that the bride is their wife and should not be taken away by another man. They feel that the bride belongs to them and so to take her away is not acceptable. The family members that the tradition classified as the *muus* are the uncles and nephews of the bride. The *muus* in the Kpelle tradition are known as the real obstacles or stumbling blocks for the groom during this ceremonial occasion. You must drive them away in the form of bribery so that you can be free to operate. We are not teaching you how to bribe folks but instead educating you on navigating your way to level the plain field in a traditional manner and form. We are encouraging you to respect and make use of our tradition and not to bypass it. And the only way to go about achieving this is to give away something valuable to the *muus* so that you can be at ease as you take on the hand of your bride.

The term *muu* is derived from the name of a traditional bird called owl in English. The Kpelle name for owl is *muu*. A Kpelle adage says that *"the best witness for witchcraft is the owl."* As you may be aware, this bird is very fearful and scary. Whenever Mr. Owl is around, people are scared or afraid to move freely because of the many perceptions and myths associated with this bird, including witchcraft. Whenever the owl bird appears in a village or town, whether by day or night, it is always driven away before the dwellers can feel free. In like manner, the groom and family must drive the uncle(s) of the bride away to get some relief as they take on the bride's hand. The uncle(s), in this case, represents the owl bird called *muu* in Jorquelleh Kpelle. Thus, the nomenclature "muu" came into the customary marriage ceremonial picture and became attached to the uncles and nephews from this background.

So, whenever you are preparing for a customary marriage within the Jorquelleh Kpelle fashion, please be aware of the *muus* so that you can take all your traditional catapult and stones to drive those birds away for you to be at ease at the ceremony. The *muus* will always make you panic or frightened as you struggle to take the hand of your bride. If you get angry and do not adequately handle the *muus* to satisfaction, I am afraid that your marital plan will automatically fail. Therefore, be patient and follow the rules of the game.

But this is the secret behind the whole thing: if you don't want to be caught in the web of traditional traps to strangulate you and want to spend a reasonable time within the ceremony, you have to drive the *muus* away, stumbling blocks to your success. The secret to drive the birds (the *muus*) away is to do your background investigation and maybe introduce a bargaining mechanism to soften your ground, or else, you may spend the whole day in the program, and you may probably end up in exasperation due to what you might term as a useless and endless delay. Since the marriage was more endogamous in the days of the old, the families of both the groom and the bride knew exactly the secrets to overcome the tradition or handle the issues easily. Since we are now marrying from diverse backgrounds, you have to be friendly with your in-laws and try to identify the *muus* you will be dealing with in the near or far future. Know the *muus* very well, especially the head muu and also the most problematic and hard-to-handle *muus*. Ask them, discuss with them ahead of the ceremony to understand your responsibilities during the ceremony as you take on their daughter's hand. Understand those tasks that may be seen as difficult and ask them to guide you. This is the traditional bribery I am talking about and not actual modern-day bribery. This bribery is about fun and the custom practice but not about stealing or embezzlement, which is a common practice in Liberia since 1847.

As the visitors' happiness increases because the engagement is accepted, the anger of the *muus* also increases. As soon as the bride accepts the engagement, the trouble for the visitors (groom & family) begins. When the token of engagement is being accepted by the bride and family, the anger of the *muus* increases because these are signs indicating that their wife is under threat to be soon taken away by another man. At this time, they will do everything possible to obstruct the ceremony traditionally. Traditional experts told us that this is the right time for the uncles and nephews to act in defiance as *muus*. Beware that quite frankly, the *muus* will try to do some things to reduce or cut off the too much happiness and handclaps of the visitors and their friends unless the tradition is fulfilled. The visitors will be compelled to go and meet the *muus*, to beg them, and even pay some money or valuable items in the form of ransom or bribery, as we earlier mentioned.

In the days of old when there was no money, experts say that valuable items like goat, sheep, cow, chicken, silver, a piece of farmland, wine, etc., were used to calm down the *muus*. A smart groom and family will not boast at this time but rather humble themselves and make big and empty promises to convince the *muus* to leave the bride with them. You have to be aware that the *muus* will pretend that they are very annoyed and do not want to talk with the visitors. But remember that these are done in a jovial manner in line with the tradition. Remember that you should have leveled the ground for yourself before the ceremony, as you were told earlier. If you are not farsighted to navigate and pave your way, the consequences will hunt you during the ceremony because some *muus* can be very tough to handle.

To level the ground means consult your in-laws and pre-bargain with them so that the traditional ground is softened for you through negotiation ahead of the ceremony. Suppose you failed to soften the ground for yourself. In that case, you will have to wear the armor of patience because this part of the program can sometimes be so irritating, tempting, boring, and very annoying, especially when you are a novice to this cultural rite. In some instances, some family members can get annoyed and threaten to leave or quit.

In the old days, the *muus* usually caught some chickens, goats, or sheep for the groom and family to pay for them or pay ransoms instead. In modern days, the *muus* can sometimes seize the microphone or other essential things to halt the ceremony. When there was no modern thing like a microphone to seize, farm animals like chickens and goats were forcibly caught by the *muus*, and the damage incurred by them would rest upon the shoulders of the visitors. In fact, they can sometimes take away the bride with anger. But remember that this is the tradition, and so don't panic but persevere.

As the *muus* mount the tension or pressure on the visitors, the groom's father or uncle will call his people for help, "*Please come and join me to beg these handsome gentlemen, our mates* (the *muus*)." After begging and spending some monies with some empty promises, the *muus* are convinced and satisfied. Finally, they agree to leave the woman (the bride) with them. This means that the visitors have intelligently driven the *muus* away to pave the way for real action.

Suppose a muu came late or later for this aspect of the ceremony. In that case, he becomes powerless because the tradition dictates that his colleagues (the *muus*) who came first will have an obligation to surely take care of him on the side instead of what is currently unfolding in our midst. But modern-day *muus* appear on numerous occasions during a customary marriage which is wrong and unacceptable. Moreover, the appearance of *muus* is just one time during a customary marriage ceremony and not on and off in the same program.

We have discovered that all *muus* are male and not female according to the tradition during our investigation to compile this manuscript. This is because the bride is constantly being chased to pick up as a wife to another home. In simple words, there is no female muu (s) found within the Kpelle tradition. At some traditional marriage ceremonies among the Kpelle people, you may or might see a bit of obstruction from the niece (s) of the groom who is marrying. This intrusion is based on jealousy. This can be done in protest so that the groom will reconsider his decision and turn around to marry her instead of the already prepared bride. The problem of the groom's niece is most often handled or taken care of the same way as the muu but in a moderate and easy-to-handle situation within a relatively shorter time.

As stated above, items like goats, chickens, cows, sheep, wine, etc., were used to beg or bribe the *muus* to go away in the old days. But the modern-day form prefers only money and nothing else. So once the *muus* are satisfied, the rocky road leading to the gowning exercise is now paved for the groom and family like the Streets of Islington in the United Kingdom.

Gowning exercise

After the *muus* are driven, peace is restored. The bride's father will then charge the groom's family to gown the bride's family (the mother-in-law & father-in-law) only. But this aspect has changed dramatically over time. Father-in-law, mother-in-law, uncles, brothers-in-law, sisters-in-law, aunties, cousins, nephews, sisters, brothers, extended family members, friends, and other dignitaries are now benefitting from the gowning exercise. In addition, the gowning is a special honor given to the biological father and mother of the bride through the presentation of specially made clothes or country cloth as gifts from the groom and family.

In some cases in the old days, the bride's grandmother and grandfather also benefitted from the gowning exercise. But today, however, grandchildren, stepchildren, brothers, sisters, even adopted children, strangers, friends, and many extended family members are now enjoying this part of the ceremony. According to our respondents, this is wrong and unacceptable to the custom because these extra participants do not have any fish to fry in this ceremonial oil as they are blind, and some of them are not yet members of the marital society. If you gowned all of these people, who then deserves this parental honor? The gowning is an honor bestowed on the bride's parents and not just anyone. Usually, the gowning is being supported by putting something like money into the pockets of each gown to add value to the honor. But because the beneficiaries of the gowning exercise are so many, nothing like money is being placed into the pocket of each gown in this era.

After the gowning exercise by this time, the dust is settled; the ground is leveled or softened, and the road is paved for the groom's family to pay the bride's price.

Remember to ensure that the *muus* are driven satisfactorily before the payment of the bride's price. This is important because it is not suitable for this aspect of the ceremony to be tempered with or interrupted as it is the happiest moment of the whole drama. Bribing and begging are the only customary solutions to break the wings of the *muus* as you were told. This approach discussed above is used when you blend the engagement and the dowry payment on the same day.

If the engagement has taken place days, weeks, months, or years before the day of dowry payment, the *muus* customarily performed after the declaration of an intent coupled with some signs that indicate the taking away of the bride. Therefore, their performance is very close to the dowry payment and partly within the dowry payment exercise. When the driving of the *muus* is done, and without any intrusion of the *muus*, the groom and family are asked to pay the dowry for the bride, which is forty-eight United States Dollars ($48.00USD). It is done in a second valuable and highly respected plate set aside for that purpose and not the same engagement plate that you used earlier for the engagement.

The Kpelle name for this $48USD is *pum-puu-kao-fayleh*. A *pum* in Kpelle is 4USD/pound, and so *pum puu kao fayleh* (12 pums or pounds) is equivalent to 40USD + 8USD, which is equal to 48USD/pound. In simple words, *pum tornor* (one pum) in the Kpelle tribe means 4 British pounds/USD in English. In modest words, since a *pum* is 4USD, you multiply 4 by 12 to obtain 48USD. Therefore, 40USD means *pum puu* (10 pums), and 8USD means *pum fayleh* (2 pums). The interpretation for this is that 10 pums + 2 pums equals 12 pums which is called *pum-puu-kao-fayleh*.

The Kpelle word for one hundred dollars ($100.00) is *whung-tornor*, while one thousand ($1,000.00) is pronounced as *walai-tornor*.

Now that you have completed the engagement exercise and that the *muus* are amicably settled, the next area of focus at the program is the dowry payment, the most attractive and interesting component of your matrimonial journey.

Chapter Five

The dowry payment

The dowry payment as a second phase of the customary marriage comes right after the engagement exercise when the muus are traditionally driven away. This is the part of the customary ceremony that you undergo as a groom to obtain your bride with a primary focus on the prescribed and required procedures. Whether you skip the space of days, weeks, months, or years after the engagement exercise or plan to do everything the same day, the dowry payment segment must always come after the engagement ceremony. Traditionally, if you complete the engagement exercise, which is the first phase, your work is incomplete without undertaking the dowry payment component. Once the process is incomplete, it is traditionally and legally dangerous for your union. And if your job to marry your bride is partial, your ownership of the bride is not complete, thus creating an avenue for conflict for a struggle over your wife-to-be. This also means that you do not have total claim or ownership of the bride that you are yearning to possess because the process is not complete.

The dowry payment entails a barrage of step-by-step activities as the tradition dictates. During the dowry payment, the bride's family normally gives the groom's family tasks to fulfill the custom. In some cases, the family can ask the groom's family to pay or provide other essential items or money before the actual dowry, $48.00USD, is paid. In many instances during such ceremony, the father or uncle of the bride who is spearheading this program normally tells the groom's parents to pay extra money or valuable item before the dowry payment because they have suffered to bring their daughter up as a child. They will insist that their daughter has been cooking, washing, cleaning up, caring for the family and the home, and doing everything for them, and so you must pay for these services since you want to take her away. As you may be aware that no one can pay back for such services, these practices add beauty to the customary marriage ceremony.

A typical Kpelle adage goes, *"The beak of a rooster does not touch the ground for nothing."* It has to take or benefit something from the ground for consumption. And so, in this case, the groom and family must give money in response to the request made by the bride's family before the process can continue. This means that such a request cannot go unnoticed; you must comply to satisfy this demand by paying something like money or other valuable items to lay this to rest.

Sometimes the groom and his people are asked, "What do you have to pay for our daughter as dowry?" When this question is asked, the floor is now open for you to go ahead. On average, the groom's family decides the value of their bride that they want to marry, although the bride's family sometimes decides the value of their daughter in other quarters of the Kpelle region. In the modern-day case scenario, most grooms usually overstep the bound of the $48.00USD by paying $50USD or above to symbolize how precious the bride is. Another reason for overstepping the $48USD bound is to boost the groom and family's morale and showcase their financial potential. In the ancient day's case scenario, specific valuable items were used to portray how precious and unique the bride was.

According to some of our contributors to this book, items like ivory, elephant tusk, leopard teeth, silver banger, gold, cow, sheep, eagle wing, and few other valuable things were used or paid as dowry in place of the $48.00USD where there was no money. A particular traditional bird called *massai-gbo-gbo*'s tail was also used for this purpose. This bird is most commonly found on the farm at the dumpsite with a long tail. I do not know precisely the western name for it. But the bird itself is very beautiful and attractive with black and white color in dominance. Even if there were monies in some instances, some grooms' families used these hard-to-find items to pay the dowry of their bride. This symbolizes the value, quality, and importance of the bride they are marrying.

Farming for the bride's family for a given period, sometimes seven years, was also another way of dowry payment, like in the case of Jacob in biblical times. In such a case, the groom's father took him to the bride's family and turned him over to work for his bride for an agreed time. In the tradition, we say, "*He is now tied to the pole/pillar of the kitchen.*" In Kpelle, we say, "He is tied to the *gili-nohn*" (kitchen pole). He is then relieved from the pole upon completion of the required task and time frame, after which his wife will be given to him through his parents. Working for the bride on her parents' farm through an agreement is the same as paying the bride's price for the bride in the days of old. It is very difficult now to see a youngster working on the farm of his in-laws as an option to pay the bride price of his bride. Money is now making headways in our traditional dowry payment as the single best option leading the way.

The dowry payment is the same as paying the bride's price. Upon request, the groom's father or representative will then instruct the custodian of the dowry, the groom's mother or aunt, to present the dowry on/in a breakable plate to the bride's father. Remember that this is the dowry and must be hand-delivered directly to the bride's father and not directly to her mother or anyone. This must not be given to the bride herself according to our custom. Unlike in the case of the engagement token, the bride's mother has the authority to receive the engagement token directly from the bride. However, the latter has the customary right to receive it first from the groom's family directly. Don't get confused. The mother or aunty or a proxy of the groom can also perform this task (delivering the dowry) depending on the arrangement. At this time, the bearer of the dowry will walk circumspectly, kneels down, and presents it to the father of the bride. The bride's father will then accept the dowry with a comment of approval after giving full traditional courtesy to his family members present. If the bride's parents are not satisfied with the amount or items given for the dowry, the groom and family members are asked to increase or improve the dowry package.

When the dowry is accepted, the groom, his father, and his mother are called up for a turnover ceremony of the bride to the visitors. By this time, the untied kola nuts are brought forward, and the bride's father will ask his daughter and the groom and family to come forward for a short time rite. In their presence, he will then instruct his daughter to take a kola nut from the engagement package and break it apart, eat it and drink a cup of water. In some cases, among the Kpelle people, the groom is also asked to eat a piece of the kola nut, and the remaining kola nuts are shared with other participants as a symbol of life, peace, love, and unity.

After this, the bride's father will request the bride to bring back the piece of kola nut that she has already eaten. The bride will typically respond that she cannot bring back or produce the piece of kola that she has eaten. Now, there is no way that a person can eat and swallow any foodstuff, including kola nut, and then bring it back the same way and condition it was in. In this case, the bride's father explains to his daughter that this is how your relationship will be difficult to go apart.

"Since it is difficult to bring back the piece of kola nut that you have eaten, so will it be traditionally impossible for you to leave, separate, or divorce your husband until death do you part." The bride's father will also explain to his daughter, *"The eating of the kola nut symbolizes the taking of oath for this union between you and this man who is marrying you today."*

Traditionally, according to traditional experts, the eating of kola nut during the customary marriage ceremony is equal to exchanging vows in Western marriage.

In a modern-day ceremony, the inclusion and eating of kola nuts into traditional marriage ceremonies have been forgotten or downplayed in many instances due to ignorance and negligence. Our careless attitudes to learning and practice the tradition cannot be overemphasized in this dispensation. But, on the other hand, most of the people who make use of the kola nut in the ceremony are doing so to raise money from the process.

Experts say that the best time to eat the kola nut is right after the dowry payment and before the turnover of the bride to the visitors. It is realized that some parents or friends and agents from the bride side are now using the inclusion of kola nuts into the customary marriage ceremony procedures all because of money, and this was not the case in the days of our forefathers. In the traditional marriage ceremony, kola nut symbolized peace, love, unity, and exchange of vows between the bride and the groom but not for money-raising technique as seen around here. In some quarters of our tradition, the kola is placed in pieces of leaves and tied countlessly. When the bride is slowly loosening the tied kola nuts in the modern-day, money is wasted on her until the process is completed.

Taking the hand of the bride versus presentation of her farewell package

After the payment of dowry and the eating of kola nut, it is now incumbent upon the bride's parents to officially turn over the bride to the groom as the tradition demands. The protocol dictates that the father or mother of the bride should take the bride's right hand and then give it to the groom's mother. In some customary quarters of marriage, the bride's left hand is used instead of the right to explain that giving the right hand out means total disconnection of the bride from her parents in that the right hand is the best and lovely hand. According to some traditionalists, the left hand is the best to give out into marriage because its fingers are directly connected to the heart, which is the symbol of love. This coincides with statutory or western marriage philosophy because it is perceived that the ring finger is on the left hand, which is connected to the heart. Some experts also say that the left hand is the best because the right hand is most often used to do many things while the left is reserved for special purposes, one of which is the customary wedding. By digging deeper into the global network through Google search, it is established that all fingers on the left and right hands are somehow connected to the heart directly (*thelist.com/162352/ the-reason-we-wear-wedding-ring-on-fourth-finger*).

Whether the right or left hand, the delivery statement is most often stated in this manner "*This is your wife for your son for life having fulfilled all aspects of the tradition.*" At this point, you can surely hear hands of applaud from the audience with joy and happiness. The groom's mother and father will then receive and give the bride's hand to her husband, the groom himself, as their son's wife for life. "*This is your wife; she is now yours from now on until death do you part. So please see her as the bone of your bones and take good care of her.*"

Traditional experts say that the best or main person to lay the bride's hand in the hand of the groom's mother is the mother of the bride with a caution that you are a mother and so, we will count on you to please take good care of our daughter. Others argue that the best person from the bride's family to give her hand out into marriage is the uncle or father. But in a day's conference held with some of our key informants, both parties said that whether the mother, uncle, or father of the bride gives the bride's hand into marriage, this does not matter. This is because an agreement is earlier reached at home as to who to lead the bride's family through this customary process. We know so far that from both families of the groom and bride, their grandparents, fathers, mothers, uncles, aunties, or the approved representatives dare to perform this ceremony on either side of the couple-to-be according to tradition.

In some cases, the groom's parents can also give the bride's hand to the groom in conclusion with a verbal warning against brutality and abuse of the woman's rights. This means that woman's rights have long been respected and recognized but on a minimum scale unknowingly. The conference also resolved that whether you give the right hand of the bride or the left hand, it does not matter that a hand is officially given into marriage. Therefore, the argument of which hand to give out into customary marriage should not be a problem because we have already lost track of some of our paths due to the lack of knowledgeable people on the subject matter. Therefore, we are encouraged to use either of the hands whenever we turn a bride over to her groom and family.

This part of the customary marriage is followed by advice from the bride's family to the groom and his family to take good care of their beloved daughter. At this point, the farewell package already prepared by the bride's family is presented to their daughter in the presence of their in-laws. The groom and family are seriously warned that with all the required items in the package, that there is no room for boasting over their daughter because she is bringing to the home "something" special, valuable and useful and not "nothing" as many married men most often say it.

Most of our KIs said that the bride did not go home along with the groom and family on that same day of marriage because she needed to stay back for better preparation and parental advice. Instead, she was usually escorted to the new home by her mother or aunty and other family members, sometimes days, weeks, or months later, instead of a modern-day bride who is immediately taken home with the groom on the same wedding day.

Now let us take a closer look at the composition of the farewell package for the bride. We are not talking about the modern-day package but rather an ancient day package here. In most instances, the bride's package contains local food-stuffs like clean or unbeaten rice, cook spoon-locally made, cassava sticks, eddoes, fanner, mortar, utensils, hoe or cut-lass, banana heads, mixed seeds, basket, etc. This is not the same as the modern-day package for the bride. On the con-trary, the so-called civilized package is enormous because of its composition intended to commensurate current realities.

I can remember the package for my big brother's daugh-ter's wedding very well when her traditional wedding was conducted at my home on July 17, 2019. The package had a rubber bowl, both plastic & stainless spoons, cook spoon, clean rice, coal pot, tub, bucket, cassava sticks, vanes of potato grains, liquor, baby diaper pin, pot, knife, banana, blanket, soap, mixed seeds, etc., which are contrary to the items of ancient days practices. Maybe this is happening because cer-tain things used in time past are no longer found in our time.

At this juncture, I want to specifically draw your attention to one of the items in the package called baby diaper pin in the modern-day case. This is because of its importance to this literary work. Modern-day family of the bride is using this item because most men, whether married or not married, are constantly telling their wives or fiancé that you did not bring a pin here into this house, and so I can kick you out anytime. Pin in this context means nothing. So, to erase the notion of *"you did not bring a pin here,"* the modern man introduced a baby diaper pin into the farewell package for the bride to close the mouths of men against this saying.

The groom and his family will then make a promise to take good care of their newly wedded woman through their family head. After these remarks, the groom takes his bride's right hand and leads her to their seats, which have been well decorated. At this time of the ceremony, the groom and his bride will sit together as husband and wife as the rest of the ceremony continues.

> *Note: this sitting together is and should be the first time in their lives because the great social wall of separation between them has now been customarily broken.*

Again, readers, this is not about modern-day customary marriage, which allows the couple to sleep together or have sexual intercourse or live together, born a child or children before their customary marriage is conducted. This sitting is referring to the real ancient time traditional practice. You might be surprised to see a couple fulfilling this custom at the age of 40, 50, 55, and 60, and even above in our generation, which was never the case. Our original traditional practice does not agree with this ideology. Living together before dowry payment was not part of the customary practice in the days of old. Our key informants lamented that if the bride and groom live together before the day of dowry payment, their action is an insult to the tradition and, therefore, should not be encouraged. If you do, you have to pay the price for such a violation, which is done at the wedding ceremony.

What else are you then honoring if you have already tasted the apple before making a request? Dowry payment is the greatest respect given to a customary wife or bride, which was done before sex. What type of respect does your bride have if you have taken or cut off the *Bel-le-ha-gbai* (virginity) before the dowry payment? *Bel-le-ha-gbai* in the Kpelle tribe means the breaking of virginity. This Kpelle terminology is most often used by the Salala Kpelle version of the Kpelle tribe. This refers to the olden day's dress code of children, inclusive of the bride. The robe was usually tied around the girl's waist and a piece of cloth hanging on it between the buttocks. This cloth was only meant to protect or cover the front or private part of the girl. If you were the first to temper with that dress code by means of sexual affairs successfully, you have broken her virginity. If the virginity of your bride is broken and not in line with the tradition, or illegal sex is committed by you, you will be charged to pay a damage fee before you can pay the dowry of your women. This is why the bride is always asked whether the *korli-kao* (dowry) is dead or alive. If she says 'no, it is dead,' this means that illegal sex has occurred. But if the answer is "yes, it is alive," then both do not know each other sexually before the day of dowry payment. And if it is dead, you are compelled to pay a damage fee of $10USD upfront apart from your official obligations because you have already bypassed the tradition.

The entire process deliberated above concludes the whole ceremony of the dowry payment before general comments are made and followed by a vote of thanks and closing remarks or prayer, if any. After that, the families usually make the closing remark of the bribe and the groom. The remarks segment begins with the groom's representative, who will thank and appreciate everyone for their support to their success. This is followed by a representative from the bride's family who will appreciate everyone for their participation and involvement in the program and then give farewell for departure.

The next thing that follows hereafter is the refreshment followed by traditional music and dances until people are exhausted. This is the time to celebrate and merit-make with the newly wedded couple. Thus, we are helping you learn how to marry traditionally and learn and practice how to maintain the custom. We are hopeful that the below chapter (chp.6) will help advise you on practicing and maintaining our customary marriage procedures for sustainability.

Chapter Six

The Sustainability of Our Customary Marriage and its Procedures

Dramatically, modern human beings are swaying away from the original customary track in terms of customary marriage's steps and procedures. To acquire the knowledge and skills on customary marriage procedures, the younger people depend on the older folks in this generation. But from several customary marriage ceremonies that we have visited, it is quite frustrating and heartbreaking to note that most of our adults and elders who should be the custodians and teachers of the tradition have forgotten or downplayed the steps and procedures that are required of the culture to get married. They have also ignored the steps and potential ingredients that value and respect the culture and tradition due to negligence. This is all because they were not eager or concerned to learn more about this part of the culture and tradition from their forefathers; they are not knowledgeable to pass it on to their children. Other key informants blamed the downward trend of the cultural practice on the careless behaviors of this and past generations.

It is not all that glitters is gold, my dear readers. Similarly, is not all silver hairs are knowledgeable on cultural and traditional matters. For you to get convinced on this assumption, try it and see. If you ask about 10 to 20 silver hairs (elders or older people), you will be surprised to see about 2% or 3% know customary marriage procedures. At the same time, the rest do not know the procedures or processes leading to customary marriage. No one in this generation is exonerated from this blame game, including myself. As I write, it is crystal clear that I have not yet taught my 29, 24, 20, and 27 years old daughters and a son some of the steps and procedures leading to customary marriage, and I surmise that you, too, are sitting with me on the same mat.

We are all responsible for the present negative paradigm shift in the tradition, specifically the customary marriage procedures. We usually put in the time to assist our children with their assignments from the classroom. But how much time do we lecture them on cultural matters? This is one reason why I agree with Chinua Achebe that things have fallen apart and that the center can no longer hold. No more moonlight dance and song, no fire hearth storytelling in the evening where some of these traditional lessons are taught or passed on to the younger people. If proper mechanisms are not put into place to arrest the situation, this may lead us to what I called a social problem of the culture and the tradition in the near future.

The farmer shows concern for their crops by asking God or praying to the gods for the rain to fall on the crops and at the same time taking practical steps to nurture, protect and care for them. For example, weeding the grass from among the crops is a practical step for sustainability. This will help the crops grow very well and yield multiple fruits for consumption and preservation for tomorrow.

As social scientists, we think that it is now time to do practical teaching to alleviate future disgrace from our children and the unborn. We must try hard not to be part of those weaklings who have failed to pass on the cultural knowledge to their children so that our offspring will not blame us tomorrow. Elders, adults, and traditionalists, please do not hold onto that special and most precious knowledge that young people need to get started. How will you be remembered that you were a reservoir of knowledge during your existence if you cannot share? We must be the game changers who should not follow the same ugly trend. If we do, this will significantly penetrate the tradition and cripple it for good. Knowledge is power, and power is greater than strength. If the young people have the knowledge needed, the culture might not fail nor fall dull. Young people must also seek knowledge and skills from knowledgeable elders to put them into practice. Seek, and you shall find, knock, and the door shall open to you.

The ants themselves know the importance of sustainability; this is why they work together as a team to stockpile their food during the dry season in preparation for the rain when it is difficult to move out in search of food. The simple logic here is that they are planning vigorously to gather enough supplies to sustain themselves for that period to avoid suffering and shortages during the heavy downpour of rain.

In this light, sustainability is vital to us in every positive thing we do, especially concerning our culture, tradition, and custom. Sustainability in this context stresses the need to teach, learn, practice, and maintain the steps and procedures of our customary marriage so that we, including incoming generations, will not forget or dash down this unique tradition.

> *"Teach a child the way he/she should grow, and when the child is old, he/she will not depart from it" (a famous biblical quotation).*

This train-the-child philosophy must be taught and practiced to resonate forever with the message of sustainability for customary marriage. Suppose we want to maintain our original steps for customary marriage. In that case, we have to teach this current generation about every critical component and protocol laid down by our great-great-grandparents and ancestors. Modern matrimony must be separated and distinct from customary marriage in the practical term. Although it may not be too bad to include some western activities or ideologies into customary marriage, but may become worst if we allow western marriage ideology to overcome ours and bury what we have already inherited. If we do, then we have not weeded the grass from among the crops so dear to us.

Let me make myself very clear here, dear readers. I am not stopping you from using some western practices in your customary marriage, but rather encouraging you to make maximum use of the tradition in your customary marriages. Maintain what you have while you add other flavors because your tradition is the foundation of your culture. For example, if you increase the farewell package for the bride more than what used to be within the ancient package, there might be no problem because some ancient items for the package are no longer found. What we met with our people should be and is the original practice and procedure to follow. A Kpelle adage says that "*before you can plait the new mat, you have to sit on the old one.*" My candid advice is that we should not dash down our custom for another one because no one will destroy their custom and replace it with ours.

The crops mentioned above are classified as our traditional or customary marriage procedures that we try to nourish. But, at the same time, the grass in the analogy represents the ills, the missteps, our negligence, and the introduction of foreign ideologies into our customary marriage procedures.

Suppose any of us thinks that I am just fabricating or making up a story about the missteps and misapplication of the procedures of our customary marriage. In that case, I will take this time to respectfully challenge you to please visit some of our traditional wedding ceremonies to prove me wrong or right. Except that you are not knowledgeable of the procedures of our customary marriage, you might indeed prove me wrong in this regard. But suppose you are actually in the know of the processes involved. In that case, you will surely understand whether the master of the ceremony during a customary marriage is on track or not. Suppose you do visit some of our modern customary marriage ceremonies. In that case, you will surely see countless mistakes covered up with consultations on the side about the steps and procedures to the extent that it may seem boring for the participants and visitors due to the prolonged delay. These consultations are done most often because people do not know how to conduct the customary marriage ceremony. And so, the consultations are done to acquire additional knowledge to help them find their way out. If you follow the western wedding, you will realize that the moderator and the clergyman responsible for spearheading and conducting the ceremony do not break and consult others to learn before they can proceed. This is because everything is on course and each one is very knowledgeable on what to do.

Some elders or people spearheading the customary marriage ceremonies sometimes do not know what to do next after specific steps or steps and must break and ask for help before proceeding. I am a living testimony to this account. When I attended more than thirteen distinct customary marriages, I was somehow compelled, if not forced, to voluntarily provide the little expertise that I have acquired from my father, some elders, and neighbors at home in Duaita, Gbarnga, and other places. I did because I saw some gaps or lapses within the process. These gaps or lapses created serious stumbling blocks or obstacles that were very embarrassing because the ceremonies could not continue due to a lack of knowledge on certain things to do at a given point in time. For example, in one of these ceremonies, the MC did not know where to start from, what to do first, second, third, or last. In another program, the MC did not know the difference between engagement tokens and dowry payment. In a third related instance, the bride's parents told the groom to pay the dowry for their daughter before gowning the bride's parents. On another occasion, there was no moderator. Instead, I saw the groom's family welcoming the bride's family with kola nuts in their own home instead of the bride's family welcoming the people from the groom's side.

Because of these above reasons and many more, I was a constraint to interfere positively in some of these hullabaloos to arrest the situations to complete the happiness of the couples and their families. Therefore, let me be very quick and bold to disclaim and proclaim that I am not an expert on the procedures of customary marriage, but rather a student who has identified some of the deficiencies and missing links within the tradition and trying to solicit the solution. Despite my support to these people at different times and venues, I am still learning the procedures of customary marriage; this is why I chose to compose this work in consultation with other old hands in the business. But also remember that *"the age of Methuselah has nothing to do with the wisdom of King Solomon."*

Digging deep is the best solution to understand what you don't know. Digging the culture deeper will help you find some social artifacts and fossils (hidden knowledge & skills) to make you an archeologist of knowledge on culture and tradition. Because we cannot speak our vernacular without mixing it up with the western language (English), this is clear evidence that we are forgetting our customary marriage procedures and abusing and downplaying our culture at every level undisputedly.

These things are happening because we have overlooked and forgotten some of our required steps due to the lack of interest in our culture and tradition. But there is a solution that lies right within our purview for these impediments, which I called viruses. But it is better late than never, as the saying goes. One philosopher said, *"Don't educate your children to be rich but teach them to be happy so that when they grow up, they will know the value of things and not the price."*

As technicians and social scientists, we think that the solution to this problem is to value what we have and have what we value. *"You will never know the importance of the shade till the tree is cut down."* To cherish what we have and have what we value is to look back to our parents, grandparents, great grandparents, and ancestors who lived before us, some of whom are still alive and willing to impart the knowledge. To look back is to consult experts and seek wisdom from people who still have grips on the custom and tradition. To consult experts means that we, the learners and custodians, must also be willing to go closer to the experts and learn, practice, and teach what we have acquired to our children and incoming generations for preservation.

Again readers, do not be complacent or sycophantic with what you have or what you've read; think outside the box and verify information concerning your tradition and cultures to enable you to teach others to uphold the tradition with references and not just utterances alone.

"*Kola nut lies in the mouth of he who values it.*" (Achebe Chinua). By interpretation, those who know the importance of the steps towards customary marriage procedures will surely learn (digging deep), pass it on and protect it from going down the drain. You could be one of those who still value this kola nut (customary marriage procedures) to join us to propagate and safeguard the message that I am proffering.

Why are you ashamed to even speak your own vernacular, your mother tongue? Do you value it to teach your children? If you are shy to speak out your own dialect among people, how can you practice your tradition and pass it on knowing that the vernacular is the center of the culture and tradition? You cannot practice the tradition without its language (the Kpelle dialect).

Dear eager readers, no one has a monopoly over knowledge. "*Two or more good heads are better than one.*" One of the most essential and valuable properties for the human race is personal knowledge. As a patriot wanting for his people and culture to benefit this property (knowledge) that they have acquired over time, he/she must teach his children, his/her followers, and others that are so dear to them. But instead of helping others to know some of what they have learned, they will hold onto the knowledge and die along with it.

This is one area where the white man has the edge over us. For them, acquiring knowledge and advancing it is a competition over knowledge to see and honor who can do it better than the other. But, on the flipped side of the coin, for us Africans, the acquisition and advancement of knowledge is a secret fraternity. For instance, we fly invisible jet planes overnight from one location to another in hidden while the white man flies his plane overnight in broad daylight for all to see and benefit from the invention. But remember, *"The evil that man does lives after him,"* said Mark Anthony at Julius Caesar's burial.

Let us glance at a short nonfictional story as narrated below concerning holding onto knowledge and skills acquired by an individual and not sharing it. A man in one of our neighboring towns in Bong County (unnamed for security reasons) had a powerful traditional medicine for severe running stomach (cholera). He used it to help heal many people but failed to teach his children or another person around him. According to the story, every time he applied the herbs, it appears like he was the one who passed on the cholera sickness to the patient because the illness will automatically stop. He was always called upon and given a token to apply the herb on victims. No one also cared at that time to be initiated for this knowledge and skill. Unfortunately, he died along with this knowledge, and that treatment ceased to exist. There was no plan for the sustainability of this knowledge. That was the end of that herbal gingerbread boy, all because of the lack of a sustainability plan.

What is the benefit then for our generation? If any of us behave like this man hereinabove, then that person is not weeding the grass from the crops but rather watering and fertilizing the grass to compete with the crops he planted. In this case, the crops will develop poorly and sometimes die amid the weeds.

In the book called Julius Caesar, Mark Anthony said, *"For we have not come here to praise Caesar, but rather to bury him."* The quotation continues, *"The evils that men do live after them, but the good ones are often interred with their bones."*

But for me, I think the other way around contrary to the above quotation. It is better to say that men's evils are often interred with their bones while the good ones live after them. I guess that I might be confusing you, but this is not the case. It is good to do good and the right things in simple terms so that it lives after you upon your death. Do not do evil to others or your generation so that the memory left behind will affect your children and their future generation. Work in a way that will allow your evil to be interred with your bone while the good side will live on for memories after you. Do not allow your evil deeds to dominate your good deeds while on earth. We will remain wicked if we learn these cultural lessons and refuse to educate those who come after us, the needy.

And so, my dear readers, we encourage you to read, conduct research and teach others for the maintenance of the steps and procedures leading to customary marriage not only for the Kpelle tribe but for any other ethnic group in Liberia. We also encourage you to copy this concept or ideology to manufacture additional manuscripts on the customary marriage procedures of other Liberian tribes. We have used this as an eye-opener to pilot and compile what you have today.

Using or advancing our ideas to write about any one of the remaining 15 tribes in Liberia will be our greatest satisfaction and reward. This will help us, and our incoming generations know and uphold all the necessary steps and procedures required to conduct customary marriage among the various tribes or ethnic groups in Liberia from one generation to another. In the end, maybe a literary scientist may emerge among us or after us to emulate our good example by compiling similar work into one book for the entire 16 ethnic groups of Liberia on customary marriage. In this way, you and I will forever be remembered in history for our works and contributions.

The practical model in the following chapter seven (7) will help you to understand, maintain and apply the prescribed procedures for customary marriage in the Jorquelleh Kpelle fashion. The model entails a practical step-by-step process as you take on that lovely hand of your bride at your marriage ceremony.

Chapter Seven

A Practical Model of Customary Marriage in the Jorquelleh Kpelle Fashion

Traditional Wedding in Liberia with Beatrice Thomas and Kollie Sonah as an example;

This chapter is designed as a model to educate readers on the practical aspect of our customary marriage procedures. The previous six (6) chapters already discussed above have given us detailed insights into customary marriage but theoretically. What matters here most in this last chapter is adherence to the various prescribed steps to follow and the practical roles of key players who are involved in the customary marriage ceremony at a particular time. Though you will slightly come across some modern features within the model, you are kindly advised to focus on the customary steps you have already acquired to apply your learning. This aspect of the book is the epicenter of our literary works. You are advised not to take it lightly because this model is the brain behind our work. The model is not a creation (make-up) but rather a real case in a real-life situation that I was fully involved with. Not only was I deeply involved, but that the model precisely summarizes the views and opinions of all our consultants, contributors, and key informants (KIs) to the entire process of the book writing. This chapter leads us from theory to the practice of customary marriage's prescribed steps and procedures among the Jorquelleh Kpelle people.

Under Liberian law, there are two main types of marriages; Traditional/customary and Statutory. A man under the traditional laws may contract multiple marriages according to traditions and customs. These marriages are legitimate and solemn under Liberian law.

A traditional marriage ceremony includes the engagement of the bride and payment of dowry to the bride's family. In most Liberian traditional marriages (TMs), the dowry consists of money and the breaking of kola nuts with other valuable items. This has made many traditionalists wrongfully conclude that it is a "payment" for the woman, and therefore, consider the woman as their property in marriage. Many people think that the caption "Bride's Price" means the selling price of the women or bride-to-be wedded. But the payment of the bride's price is simply the fulfillment of custom and not the buying price for the human being called the bride. As being human is different from human being, the payment of the bride's price is also different from the buying price in the market. Have you ever seen a groom paying for the bride during a western marriage? The answer is 'no' because there is no price for a woman to include the bride. Traditional marriages last until death or divorce. The requirements for divorce within the tradition typically follow prescribed traditions.

The practical case below here has touched and inspired me to use it as an example amongst many customary ceremonies that I have witnessed and participated in based on the closeness of the customary picture we envisage or visualize for our use, including my readers.

Beatrice's case:

Getting Started

On December 31, 2020, a traditional marriage rite was performed between Beatrice Thomas and Kollie Sonah. Madam Musu T. Cammue and Davidson Sumo served as the mother and father to Beatrice at the wedding. Beatrice Thomas and Kollie Sonah were the bride and groom at the wedding. On the other hand, George Phillip Mulbah and Ma Gorpu Sonah served as the uncle and mother to Kollie for this customary marriage. Abednego Cammue and Moses Tear Cammue played the roles of the muus for this wedding. So you might see the names of these actors seldom or most often throughout the whole episode as things unfold.

Formalities during the traditional wedding ceremony

It all started with the singing of traditional songs and traditional dance performances. The place was well decorated with seating capacity organized. The decoration of the venue was dominated by traditional items and designs like green banana, calabash, fresh bitter-ball, yam, rice on straws, potato grains, and more, all hanging in and around the scaffold. The western decoration was also visible in some corners of the platform. Balloons and imported flowers were some of the components of western decoration. The family of the bride and the groom, friends, and well-wishers, all in attendance, singing and dancing, showing a great deal of love and happiness for the anticipated union of the couple.

According to our customs and traditions, it is the responsibility of the bride's uncle to give his niece's hand out into marriage; on the other hand, the uncle of the groom is charged with the responsibility to find a wife for his nephew. On this note, the declaration of intent during Kollie's traditional wedding ceremony was made by his uncle, Mr. George Phillip Mulbah, who served in the capacity of the father. On the other side of the river, Davidson Sumo served as the father for Beatrice. Remember that the tradition in our case can allow either the father or uncle and mother or aunty of both the groom and the bride to perform this task for each family in addition to the biological parents of the bride and groom.

Davidson began by welcoming the groom's family and the rest of the participants to the ceremony. He introduced himself first and key family members, including their functions. Next, he gave the ceremony overview and then asked the groom's family to introduce people and their tasks for the occasion. He also called on the representative of the groom's family to state their purpose of visit and then took his seat.

George Phillip Mulbah rose and introduced himself and his family members, including their status or functions within the family. He then openly announced the purpose of the visit, and this is what he said, *"I saw a beautiful lady here in your home and have come to ask her hand into marriage to my son."*

This declaration is quite correct to be replicated for our use, and we encourage you to follow suit.

Beatrice's Uncle: *You said that you had seen a beautiful lady here, but we don't know who you are talking about! What is her name?*

Kollie's Father: *Well, her name is Beatrice Thomas.*

Bride's Uncle: *Well, that is fine, but I have many Beatrice here and don't know which one of them you are talking about. So I will allow you to look around this gathering and point out the princess you have come to marry. When you see the one you are talking about then, you should please let me know.*

This part of the occasion was full of fun and entertainment as the bride's family gave the go-ahead, searching for Beatrice to choose multiple-choice selections among the women.

Kollie's Father: *Let me walk around and look for the Beatrice that I am talking about. This is Beatrice, the woman that I am talking about.*

He pointed at her from a distance without touching because it is not permissible to touch the bride at this time according to the tradition unless the process is completed.

Note: Money was never raised or paid for the searching at this time. There was no special covering of false brides using lappa, no parade of brides, and no money requested.

In the case of western marriage, the search is done at what we called shower night. This customary search concludes the introductory part of the ceremony, thus leading us to part one of the customary marriage processes, which is the bride's engagement.

Part I: The engagement exercise

By this time, the bride in question is found and is brought forward and well seated flat on a mat already prepared for her. Traditionally, this mat must be spread by the family of the groom.

> **Beatrice's Uncle**: *Mr. Moderator, please tell our guests that we are now ready. Let them take the stage and go ahead to perform what they have come for.*

At this time, the moderator called for order and gave the stage to the visitors to engage their bride. All eyes are set on the stage, watching with eagle eyes.

> **Kollie's Uncle**: *This is the plate with the token of engagement. Ma Nowai (mother of the groom), please take it to Beatrice and tell her that we want her hand into marriage to our son, Kollie.*

Kollie's mother walked cautiously and knelt before Beatrice and presented the plate with the same instruction given to her.

> **Kollie's Mother***: This is your engagement Beatrice, we want your hand into marriage to our son.*

Remember that the engagement plate is directly handed to the bride herself first from the hands of the groom's representative who is doing the presentation. And so, Beatrice received the token and took it to her mother. She walked carefully and also knelt respectfully as she presented the engagement in this manner.

> **Beatrice***: Mother, I received this engagement package from our visitors that they want me to be a wife to their son.*

> **Beatrice's Mother***: I have received it, daughter, but what do you say to the proposal from our guests? They say that they want you to marry their son.*

> **Beatrice***: Yes, mother, I do accept and agree to the proposal willingly with all my heart. Yes, I accept and agree.*

Beatrice is told to take her seat. There were more handclaps and laughter.

> **Beatrice's Mother***: My mothers, sisters, aunts, all concerned, this is what our child has received, and we need your blessing so that I can carry it to her father.*

She paused and got some responses like, oh yes, it's a good thing, we agreed, go ahead. She continued.

> **Beatrice's Mother**: *My husband, I received this engagement from our daughter. She has willingly accepted the request made to her for marriage. It reaches you as the father.*

> **Beatrice's Father**: *My wife, our daughter has agreed, and our people have endorsed, and so I submit. Let us go ahead. I do agree unconditionally.*

At this time again, you could hear loud hands of applaud and endless laughter with happiness because the odds favor the groom and family. This happiness and hand claps caused the muus to get annoyed that another man wants to take away their wife. But at this point, the muus must be patient to wait for the dowry payment before performing. This is because the engagement and dowry payment were not made together in the days of old. And so, the muus did not perform in the first phase (the engagement phase) but instead performed in the dowry payment phase, which is the second part of the process. And so, the muus waited for the dowry payment segment to perform accordingly.

Another formality that followed was the loosening of the kola nut. The groom's family has already tied pieces of kola nut in a bundle of leaves using a very tiny thread or rope wrapped around the leaves many times and placed them into the engagement plate.

Beatrice's Father: *Please loose the thread or rope from the kola nuts very slowly and carefully.*

During this time, money was also being offered but not compelling nor asked for. When she finally finished, the kola nuts were kept on the table inside the engagement plate, waiting for the appropriate time, the second phase of the process.

Part II: The practical dowry payment

Now everyone is again attentive and ready to witness the second and final phase of the process, which is the primary action area of the ceremony, the dowry payment. As these formalities went on, the visitors were very boastful that money was not their problem.

"We are ready if it's money, we will pay because we came very prepared," they said.

This is meant for fun anyway, so don't get angry with your guests (the groom's family). These are some of the beauties of the customary marriage drama. The bride's family should not take this against the groom and his family because these are things that add value to this cultural practice.

As the visitors were preparing to conduct the dowry payment, the muus were already angry and in action because of the statement contained earlier in the open declaration of intent concerning their woman. They took hold of the entire show, seized the microphone, and even halted the ceremony. Be aware that nothing can now go on unless the muus are peacefully and traditionally driven away using your symbolic traditional catapult and stones (your intuition to bargain).

Two muus at this occasion then seized the bride in question and planned to take her away with anger. But remember that this is the tradition and so don't panic. You need to pay a ransom now, or else your bride may get missing in action. And if this happens, your participants or audience may reduce in number or get irritated. And so, be focused and quick to put things under control. Novices to this part of the tradition can most often get annoyed and threaten to leave the program. But please do not go away because this is not extraordinary outside of the tradition, but it is just one of the many scenes you have to witness or undergo.

> **Kollie's Father**: *My family members, please come, fill my pockets with more money and join me to beg these handsome gentlemen, our mates. Don't allow them to carry our bride away.*

He then spent some money very quickly along with his people and convinced the muus, and finally, they agreed to leave the stage and the embattled woman (the bride) with the groom's family. This means that he has intelligently and peacefully driven the muus away to pave their way for real action. But the battle with these muus was not very tough to handle because these muus were a bit moderate as compare with muus of other ceremonies. Beware that some muus can be very stubborn, hard-headed, and problematic. But remember, the patient dog eats the fattest bone. Since you don't know the type of muus you might deal with in the future, and please investigate and introduce a bargaining system to level the traditional ground for yourself, as you learned in previous chapters.

Kollie's Uncle: *This is the dowry, Ma Nyamah, my wife, take it and give it to Beatrice's uncle.*

Remember that the plate bearing the dowry must be hand-delivered directly to the father/uncle of the bride at this time, unlike in the case of the engagement token.

As Kollie's mother took the first step forward, Beatrice's uncle said to her;

Beatrice's Uncle: *Hold on yet, Mother, you have some obligations to fulfill before that special ceremony is performed. Do you see this big basket? You people have to fill it with money before proceeding because you are about to take away my only daughter, who has been doing everything for us. Comfort us before you pay her dowry. Fill this basket and fill my pocket with money before you can do your thing.*

Kollie's Uncle: *Ok, in-law, that is not a big problem. Money is not the problem here today, as we said.*

He called his followers to put in some monies in the basket, pretending that it is filled.

Beatrice's Uncle: *(*looking into the basket*), You have not done anything yet, my people, so you are not ready yet to marry the woman you want.*

Then, he sat down quietly and turned his back to the stage. He even walked away, pretending he was using his phone.

Kollie's Uncle: *What is money? Please come and see. We are all ready to fill this basket.*

He and his people added up more money and retook their seats. This aspect went on for a couple of minutes until the bride's family was satisfied or felt sorry for their visitors. At this juncture, the actual dowry payment began. Again, all eyes and ears opened, mouths closed, and fingers crossed for the actions.

Kollie's mother walked traditionally and knelt before the bride's father and presented the dowry to him.

Kollie's Mother: *We said that we are ready, and so this is the dowry that I brought for Beatrice on behalf of my family.*

Beatrice's Father: *Thank you, Mother, we accept the dowry.*

He said this after informing his family members about the dowry that he has received for their daughter. In many instances, at this point, the recipient of the dowry usually consults or informs the dignitaries of the family. In our Liberian context, we say *hang-head*. This is done to give honor to all stakeholders from the bride's family. In some cases, the father or uncle of the bride accepts the dowry without consultation. He then delivered it to Beatrice's mother as the custodian until family discussions are held later.

As a reader, your assignment here is to find out how to do a traditional walk on such occasions as stated above. Please be reminded that the bride has no decision to make on how the family uses or apportions the money raised from the dowry payment as wrongly perceived in some quarters of our tradition. The dowry is directly hand-delivered to the father or uncle of the bride and not the bride herself neither the mother.

Beatrice's uncle moved to the center of the gathering.

> **Beatrice's Uncle**: *Beatrice, please come closer along with our in-laws and the groom. Take a piece of the kola nuts and eat it.*

He also shared the remaining kola nuts with the rest of those around, including the groom.

> **Beatrice's Uncle**: *Beatrice, please return the kola nut to me that you have eaten.*

> **Beatrice**: *No, Father, I am sorry. I am not able to bring it back because I have already chewed and swallowed it, and it has gone into my stomach.*

> **Beatrice's Father**: *I knew you would surely say this, Daughter. This is how it should be difficult to divorce, separate, or leave your husband until death do you part according to the tradition. The eating of the kola nut is the symbol of oath for this union between the two of you. Bring your hand, my Daughter*

Beatrice." (He took her right hand and gave it to Kollie's mother for onward passage to the groom's uncle.) *This is your woman for life. We give you our daughter's hand into marriage to your son instead of the father (your husband) because you are a mother. We will depend on you for good care that you usually provide to your children. So take her along with you upon your departure as you have diligently and respectfully fulfilled the custom of the Kpelle people. Thank you.*

After this rite, Kollie received the hand of Beatrice from his parents and led her to their seats, separately for them, which had been prepared and well decorated. Then, as they sat side by side, the finishing formality of the ceremony continued.

Presentation of the farewell package

When the newly wedded couple had taken their respective seats, the bride's representative came forward and took center stage to bid farewell to their daughter as she prepared to go to her new home. We have already given you some details about this package, and it's the summary presented to you here. I have already told you what the farewell package contains in the days of old and modern days. The presentation of this package can be done by either the bride's father/uncle or the mother/aunty. Some traditional experts on customary marriage also said that a proxy can present this farewell package on behalf of the bride's family based on the arrangements and agreement among family members. The farewell is about the pouring of blessing on their daughter and giving strong warnings to their in-laws against maltreatment of their child in her new home away from her parents' home.

In this ceremony, Beatrice's father was the representative who cautioned the groom and offered the package to their daughter. And so the farewell package and the blessing were delivered by Beatrice's uncle and aunty in this manner.

Beatrice Uncle: *Do you see any bruise or broken limbs on our daughter's body? Did we call you or force you to come and marry our daughter? Are you taking her hand in the street or from her home?*

The Groom: *No, sir, I am taking her from her parents' home, and there are no bruises or broken parts of her body. My parents and I were not forced nor called to come and marry your daughter. We did the search and decided to marry her; it's not your fault, we decided.*

Beatrice's Uncle: *Ok, young man or son. Well answered. Please respect her value like yourself. Don't beat on her. Bring her back peacefully and respectfully when you are tire of her love. Give us her complaint when she goes wrong. Do you see her package? Do not tell her in your life that she did not bring anything into your home because her package contains good and valuable assets that she brings to you. In this package, there were clean rice, potato greens vanes,* *dishes and utensils, mortar, fanner, baby diaper pin, tub, knife, broom, cassava sticks, etc. The package was very big. There was a particular item in this package that needs to be emphasized. This item is included in the package. The baby diaper pin in the package is intended to prove that she is bringing something home. Do not tell her that she never brought a pin here in your life.*

Beatrice's Mother: *My daughter, Beatrice, please do not make us shame as family. Respect your husband and his family members. Remember that the man is the head of the home; take good care of him, feed him, and make him happy. Remember that we are giving you to only one man and not two or more. Please keep the torch burning for your family. May our ancestors of the land bless you, protect you and help you to prosper in life. May God help you to reproduce after your kind. Thank you, my daughter. You can now go in peace.*

This blessing concludes the entire customary marriage process from start to finish.

Before the wedding celebration, a space was created for the visitors to make a special remark from the groom's family, which was done through the groom. The groom's father, uncle, or representative is also allowed to remark. He thanked everyone for their support and participation in the program and unleashed countless blessings on all for their great success.

After that special remark, the vote of thanks was done by Beatrice's uncle in this manner; *"On behalf of the bride and family, I want to say many thanks and appreciations to all of you for your financial and moral support to us from the start of this program to finish. May God bless you all and replenish what you have spent. See you next time."*

Upon the words thank you and see you next time, the grand celebration commenced with food, drinks, songs, and traditional dances until the wee-wee hours (late hours of the night). There is no particular formality for this other aspect of the ceremony that I know because everyone is going their way and doing things their own way. There is no control, no law, and no order by this time that I know to help me send you a clearer picture of what to do and what not to do at this time.

There is no fixed formula given to me to use for such a customary marriage ceremony celebration. This is because our key informants could not give us a fixed formula or pattern during the data collection period of our work. You can design your style of celebration for your traditional wedding if you can. The most common celebration in the old days is to beat country drums, dance, drink, and eat. Some of our key informants told us that there is no special formula for such a play. Therefore, dancing, singing, drinking, eating, etc., become the order of the day.

For the modern-day celebration, most often used is a PA system usually mounted with musical sets, playing musical instruments, while people are dancing, drinking, and eating.

I can tell you here that when things are settled, some family members of the bride can join hands with the groom's family to escort the bride home. And when this is successfully done, the final whistle of the ceremony is blown, meaning everything is over, and that becomes the end of the traditional gingerbread boy. Whether you go home or not as a spectator or stakeholder, the game of marrying traditionally is over. This is how our forefathers took the hand of their loved ones in the days of old.

In ancient times, the bride did not go home with the groom on the same day of the wedding. Instead, she was usually escorted a few days, weeks, or months later by her parents or family members into the new home. Therefore, let us read, ask people and share relevant information among us so that this and incoming generations will have access to our tradition, the custom, and the culture of our dear ethnic group.

Let us learn, practice, value, and uphold what we have according to Lord Macaullay's address to the British parliament on Feb. 2, 1835; "(... for if the Africans think that all that is FOREIGN and ENGLISH is good and greater than their own, they will lose their self-esteem, their native culture and they will become what we want, a truly dominated nation)".

Thank you for reading, as reading makes one wiser.

Epilogue

Our culture and tradition are evidently fading away with terrific speed. The original or prescribed procedure for customary marriage as one of the components and ingredients of the culture is seriously at the verge of collapse. The everyday use and practice of our customary marriage procedures are waning down and being swept under the carpet by you and me all because of the introduction of western ideologies, self-denial, our idleness, negligence, copy and paste ideology, abandonment of our vernacular, unwillingness to learn and teach others, and many more vices. The death of our customary marriage procedures is very close to the grave because we have suffocated it for so long and in many diverse ways. The original concepts and procedures are gradually eroding because of our lackadaisical attitudes. If it does, our children and incoming generations will open a new chapter of culture because the original prescribed ones will no longer be available for them to use.

Currently, there is a social problem of brain-drain in our midst to provide needed information about the tradition. The tradition is crying from death at the hospital of culture. It is only you and I that have the therapeutic solutions to get it back on its feet. Digging deeper into the culture and passing on the knowledge to others is the road or conduit to resuscitate the fainted culture back on track. This is not just limited to the Jorquelleh Kpelle tribe, but to the rest of the 16 tribes in Liberia.

And so, readers please join me, let's get started today and not tomorrow. It might be too late if we wait for the next minute or hour to safe our culture.

Author

Davidson Sumo was born unto the union of Mr. & Mrs. Isaac Sumo on October 10, 1972, at the Du-Side Hospital some miles away from Monrovia, the nation's capital. He is the 3rd of 10 children (4 sons & 6 daughters). His father was traditionally inclined but later converted to Christianity. His mother, Ma Gorpu Sumo, was a devoted Christian who sang in the Kpelle dialect choir in the Baptist setting. Thus, Davidson and his siblings grew up in a Christian home.

Mr. Sumo started his early childhood education in 1980 in Duaita, his father's hometown. He moved to Tappita, Nimba

County, in 1984, where he attended the Dr. Taryor Elem. & Jr. high School under the guidance of his senior Sister, Rebecca M. Gbelee, and her husband. He also attended the Christian High School there until grade eight before his departure for LAC Grand Bassa County in 1987. Davidson completed his junior high education at the St. Joseph Catholic School in 1991 in LAC, Grand Bassa County.

In 1996 after the Liberian Civil War, he returned home with his parents. He later enrolled at the St. Martin Catholic Community high School in Gbarnga City, where he began his secondary education. A year later, he entered the Dolokelen Gboveh High School in Gbarnga City, Bong County. Davidson completed his secondary education there in 1999.

After working for thirteen years as a social worker, Davidson enrolled at Cuttington University in mid-2013, located in Suakoko District, Bong County. He was a self-sponsored student throughout his academic sojourn at the nation's most prestigious university. As a social worker, Davidson used a considerable chunk of his earnings to pay his fees at the university where he studied Public Administration, emphasizing Peace & Development Studies. He completed his studies on August 4, 2017, with honors, as magna cum laude, earning a Bachelor of Arts degree in Public Administration. In the same year, Davidson continued his studies at LICOSESS Teacher Training College, completing his thesis to earn a "B" Certificate in Teacher Training at Goll Farm Community in Bong County. During this time at the college, he served as the second student council president. In addition, Davidson advocated for transferring the college's branch to Gbarnga, the provincial capital of Bong County, in the same year.

Mr. Sumo has undergone much training ranging from Standard First Aid, disaster management, teacher training, human rights, vulnerability capacity assessment, KAP survey, behavior change communication, Participatory Rural Appraisal, DELTA, etc. His acquired knowledge and skills are from local, national, and international institutions, including the Liberia Agricultural Company, Liberian Red Cross, Medicine Du Monde, Lutheran Development Service, CHESS-Liberia, and Development Education Network-Liberia (DEN-L), amongst others. In addition, he loves extensive reading and writing based on his philosophy that reading makes a person wiser.

Davidson Sumo is married to Nancy G. Sumo, and they are blessed with four children; Priscillia, Jonah, Susan, and Amanda.

Appendix

Equal Rights of Customary Law of Liberia, 1998 & 2003. An Act to Govern the Devolution of Estate & Establish Rights of Inheritance for Spouses of Both Statutory and Customary Marriage, approved Oct. 7, 2003 & published Dec. 1, 2003,

The 1986 Constitution of Liberia chapter 3 Articles a & b, Chapter 22 Articles a & b.

Macaullay's address to the British Parliament, 1835, *Page 125*

Julius Caesar, McAnthony - The evils that men do." *Page 105*

Map of Liberia

Bong County Flag

Abbreviations

KIs- Key Informants
CM- Customary Marriage
TM- Traditional Marriage

Glossary

Bellehagba: Kpelle term for the break of virginity by bringing down the first cloth covering the girl's private parts for sexual pleasure for the very first time

Bride's price: $48USD or the equivalent services given or paid to own a bride

Culture: the way of life of certain group of people

Custom: the practice or institution through which traditions are practiced and upheld

Customary Marriage: *<also known as traditional marriage>* is a process through which a male and a female come together as husband and wife through a special ceremony performed locally among a particular group of people, tribe, nation, and region

Doomsday: referred to the end of the world or judgment day

Double-marriage: a couple who got married twice *<customarily & statutorily>* based on traditional and legal grounds.

Dowry: traditional token ($48.00USD) usually paid for the bride by the groom in fulfillment of custom. *<also called the bride's price>*

Endogamous marriage: marriage within the same family, social group, same tribe, same region, etc.

Engagement: a traditional package given through traditional processes to engage the bride that you want to marry

Exogamous marriage: marriage outside the family, social group, same tribe, region, and so on.

Farewell package: bundle containing assorted valuable items given to the bride for use in her new home as a form of empowerment

Gilinoh: the poles or pillars that hold the country kitchen *<outside shed used for cooking>* from falling

Homosexual: a person who is sexually attracted to people of their own sex. *<male counterparts who practice and live in same sex marriage>*

Inevitable: unavoidable or predictable phenomenon or circumstance that is most likely exists or about to occur

Key Informant: interviewee who contributed to the collection of important information on customary marriage procedures during this project

Korli-kao: the Kpelle term for dowry or bride's price

Lappa: a colorful wrapper/garment widely worn in West Africa by women. *<the formality of the wrapper depends on versions and varies from simple draped clothing to fully tailored ensembles>*

Lesbian: a gay/homosexual woman *<female partners engaged in the practice of sexual affairs between women>*

Marriage: a process through which a man shall leave his father and mother and cleave unto his wife, and they shall become one flesh

Massai-gbogbo: traditional black and white color bird usually found at the dumpsite on the farm

Muus: the uncles and nephews of the bride commonly known as owners of the woman

Pum tornor: Kpelle term for one British pound or one US Dollar in ancient days

Shillen tornor: Kpelle term for twenty cents which derived from the British currency in ancient days

Shilling: name of the British currency

Tradition: a belief, custom, practice, institution, etc. of a particular group of people in a given area

Transgender: a person whose sense of personal identity and gender does not correspond with their birth sex. *<the extraction and transplanting or replacement of a genital organ with an opposite one through surgical means based on informed consent>*

Visitors/guests: the combination of the groom, the father, mother, siblings, extended family members, friends and well-wishers attending the ceremony from the side of the groom during a traditional marriage ceremony

Welli-kao: Kpelle term for the engagement token

Western Marriage: the modern form of marriage that brings together a male and a female into one union with religious and legal backings. *<also called statutory or civil marriage>*

Xenophobic: intolerant act or racial discrimination against a particular group or class of people based on their language, tribe, color, vulnerability status, etc.

Bibliography

Achebe, Chinua. n.d. Things Fall Apart.

Champion, Justine. n.d. The Parts of a Book for Self Published Authors.

Dolo, Peter S. n.d. Mano script writer, interview on pronunciation and meaning of the word BUT, Gbarnga, Bong County

Encyclopedia Britannica. 2020.

Jenkins, Jerry J. n.d. How to Write a Book for Beginners From Start to Finish.

Johnson, Kesselly. n.d. Lorma elder, interview on pronunciation and meaning of the word BUT, Gbarnga, Bong County

Konneh, Dolomark. n.d. Gola Governor, interview on pronunciation and meaning of the word BUT, Gbarnga, Bong County

n.d. Liberia-people/Britannica.

Momo, Alfred J. T. n.d. Kru elder, interview on pronunciation and meaning of the word BUT, Gbarnga, Bong County

PhD, Amos Sawyer. 1986. The constitution of Liberia.

Siakor, Franklin O. n.d. Chief Editor

n.d. Thelist.com/162352/the-reason-we-wear-wedding-rings-on-fourth-finger.

The Liberian Legislature. An Act to Govern the Devolution of Estates & Establish Rights of Inheritance for Spouses of both Statutory and Customary Marriage of 1998. n.d.

n.d. Trans/andro/.2019jun., Benjamin, 1964.

n.d. Wikipedia,Guide.com. www.sociology.

n.d. www.vocabulary.com.

Editorial Board

Hon. Franklin O. Siakor - *Chief Editor*; Founder, Development Education Network-Liberia (DEN-L); Lecturer, Cuttington University, Liberia

Professor John Y. Gormuyor - *Lecturer*, Cuttington University, Liberia

Contributors/Key Informants

- Alhaji Sekou Sirleaf (*Elder/Traditionalist*) Ganta Parking, Gbarnga, Bong County
- Earnest Siakor (*Elder/Traditionalist*) Samay Town & Gbarnga, Bong County
- John F. Locula (*Clan Chief, High Priest/Traditionalist*) Suakoko Town, Bong County
- Kerkulah Nuatomue (*Traditionalist*) Galai & McGill Towns, Bong County
- Kweellegbo Kapu (*Former Bong County Education Officer, Traditionalist*) Gbarnga City & Galai Town, Bong County
- Ma Gorlikawuan (*Traditionalist*) Foloblai Town, Bong County
- Ma Korto (*General Town Chief*) Wainsue Town, Bong County
- Mulbah Sulonteh (*Deacon, Traditionalist*) Gbarnga, Bong County
- Mulbah T. Jacob (*Elder*) Gbenequelleh Town, Bong County
- Nyamah Nanhnon (*Traditionalist*) Duaita & Gbarnga, Bong County
- Paul K. Ricks (*Elder, Writer & Lecturer*) of Kpelle language at Cuttington University, Suakoko, Bong County.
- Sunday T. Mulbah (*Pastor, Traditionalist*) Suakoko Town, Bong County
- Timothy K. Morris (*Elder & Traditionalist, Evangelist, Barta*) Sheansue Clan & Gbarnga, Bong County

Index

Connect With Author

Readers of this book are encouraged to contact
Mr. Sumo with comments:
Email: davidsonsumo76@gmail.com

Visit author's Facebook page:
www.facebook.com/sumo.davidson

Village Tales Publishing provides traditional publishing services and turnkey services to individuals that seek to successfully self-publish and promote their books. We handle all aspects of publishing; editing, cover design, production, marketing and order fulfillment.

Please visit our websites:
www.villagetalespublishing.com
www.oass.villagetalespublishing.com

Join our mailing list for updates on new releases, deals, bonus content, and other great books from Village Tales Publishing.

Email Us:
villagetalespub@gmail.com
info@villagetalespublishing.com
****

Like Us on Facebook
www.facebook.com/villagetalespublishing
Follow Us
@villagetalespu

www.ingramcontent.com/pod-product-compliance
Lightning Source LLC
Chambersburg PA
CBHW060236030426
42335CB00014B/1483